bright bazaar

BRIGHT BAZAAR

PHOTOGRAPHY
BY ANDREW BOYD
TRAVEL PHOTOGRAPHY
BY WILL TAYLOR

jacqui
small

BRIGHT BAZAAR

EMBRACING COLOUR FOR MAKE-YOU-SMILE STYLE

WILL TAYLOR

First published in 2014 by
Jacqui Small LLP
An imprint of Aurum Press
74–77 White Lion Street
London N1 9PF

PUBLISHER: Jacqui Small
ASSOCIATE PUBLISHER: Joanna Copestick
MANAGING EDITOR: Lydia Halliday
ART DIRECTION AND STYLING: Will Taylor
LOCATION RESEARCH: Will Taylor
DESIGN: Smith & Gilmour
EDITOR: Sian Parkhouse
PRODUCTION: Maeve Healy
**ENDPAPER ICONS AND BRIGHT.BAZAAR
LOGO DESIGN:** Amanda Jane Jones

ISBN: 978-1-909342-20-0

A catalogue record for this book is
available from the British Library.

2016 2015 2014
10 9 8 7 6 5 4 3 2 1

Printed in China

FLORAL FANCY (page 1) A blue vase
arranged with freshly cut pink blooms
and foliage serves as a pretty accent
point to the lime green walls of Raina
Kattleson's American living room.

PRIVATE VIEW (pages 2–3)
This industrially flavoured Copenhagen
warehouse bedroom makes a statement
with an eye-catching gallery wall of
sporting-themed art prints and paintings.

WONDERFULLY WHIMSICAL
(front jacket) A trio of graphic pattern,
whimsical prints and block brights
harmonize to create a colourfully
eclectic vibe in the living room of
Will Taylor's London flat.

*This book is dedicated to Toby and Gran,
who never fail to make my life colourful,
even when skies are grey.*

★ BB ★ CONTENTS

I'm just a gentleman hooked on hue...

Colour is at the very heart of my life; it's the foil that brings light and shade, depth and interest to my everyday experiences. Whether it's the cheerful blue and yellow post boxes I saw on a trip to Stockholm, or the graphic contrast of New York City's yellow taxicabs against the city's otherwise monochromatic palette of skyscrapers and sidewalks, it's the colour in these moments that always sits at the heart of my memories and inspires my decorating palettes. It's fair to say I've always been a palette addict. Are you?

As I write I'm sat in the late-afternoon sun dappling the courtyard at a small chateau in Provence, France. The sun's rays are warming my back; the quiet buzz of bees in the surrounding lavender and gentle splashing of a fountain my only company. The wrought-iron table and chairs I'm sitting at are nestled amongst a lavender bed, which is swaying in the occasional breeze. The mauve buds of the lavender drench the courtyard in a sea of purple, which is the perfect contrast to the weathered and faded ochre walls of the building behind. It's a cherished moment of calm where I can appreciate the natural beauty that colour brings to our world — the perfect catalyst to inspire a new decorating palette.

Colour doesn't only inspire me in idyllic locations; it is also a source of comfort during troubled times. I was only eleven years old when I arrived home from a friend's house to find that my dad had left home without warning or saying goodbye. As a young boy my world turned upside down, because until that point I had been lucky enough to know only the security of a happy family life: joyful holidays to Greece and Portugal with my dear gran in toe, and camping out in my brother's bedroom on Christmas Eve for what felt like an eternity, waiting for the clock to strike six so that we could open our presents at the foot of our parents' bed. The subsequent experiences were often beyond my years, but they taught me to grow up quickly. And although times were hard, I now look back and see how I sought solace through colour without realizing I was doing so. Just like my wide-eyed wonder at my first sight of the azure blue Mediterranean Sea on family holidays, and the comforting saffron yellow and orange lick of flames in the fireplace on Christmas morning, I had continued to find joy in colour during harder times. Waking up in my sunflower yellow bedding and opening my true blue window blind to see the lush green fields across the road were comforting

ADDING A DASH OF
COLOUR TO A SNOWY
PARIS SCENE!

It's your memories that tell the story of your personal connection to hue.

reminders that my bedroom still felt like home, no matter how difficult things were.

I fondly remember the colours of a walk I took with my gran and her dog Bruno one morning on our first Christmas without dad. We were all adjusting to how the traditions we had always known were changing, so it was great comfort to head out into the countryside. It's the colours I saw on that walk that pierce my memory most strongly: we admired the way the red berries popped against the winter landscape, breaking off branches to take home for mum to cheer her day; the sparkle of the ice blue frost that crunched reassuringly under foot; and how we both laughed as we struggled over the weathered yellow farm gates.

As an adult, colour continues to bring confidence and joy to my life – I love how wearing a brightly coloured watch or bow tie makes me feel ready to take on the day ahead. But nothing betters coming home to a colourful space that feels like a true reflection of my personality. And that leads me onto why I've written this book – I hope that it will not only encourage you to value colour in all of life's experiences, but inspire you to use colour to make your home a true reflection of you and your life. After all, colour is highly personal, so it's the perfect element to help make your house feel like a home. Take a moment to think about the key events in your life; picture where you were and what you were doing. Perhaps it's the array of hues in the flowers on your wedding day, the colour of your first car or the cheerful crocheted blanket that didn't leave your side when you were a child. Whatever the event, it's your memories that tell the story of your personal connection to hue. My hope is that the Bright.Bazaar book will lead you to discover your perfect palette and inspire you to decorate with those hues at home.

The book progresses in three sections, each aimed at helping you create a palette that's personal to you, as well as arming you with the colour confidence to decorate your home in a vibrant and uplifting style that's bursting with personality. The first, Colour Is Your Friend, is an introduction to the Bright.Bazaar take on colour, as well as a mix of quick and inspiring ways to invite more colour into your home that you can try today. Think of this as the courting period, where each new colour idea is a date for you to find your rhythm in your personal relationship with hue. Next is Colour Cocktails, where I show you intriguing ways to discover the colours you like best and how to transform your everyday colour inspirations into stylish and vibrant colour palettes, which are demonstrated by my personal inspiration pictures as well as vivid and energetic spaces from homes across the world. In the final section, Bringing Colour Home, I explore how to invite colour into every room in your home and make it work for you. Throughout the book I've included 'Will's Colour Secrets' – nuggets of helpful colour know-how so that it feels like we're on this bright and colourful journey together. Paintbrushes at the ready? It's time to get hooked on hue!

Will Taylor

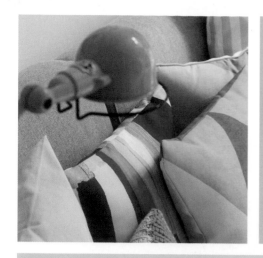

COLOUR IS YOUR FRIEND

QUINTESSENTIALLY COLOURFUL

Are you dubious about the thought of bringing colour into your home? Or maybe you'd like to try layering some splashes of colour into your rooms but just don't know where to start? Either way, this chapter is designed to introduce you to the Bright.Bazaar approach to decorating, outline ways to build your confidence in using colour and give examples of quick-win colourful decorating ideas that will give your scheme an instant wow factor. Whether it's painting the front door in your favourite hue or giving a tired piece of furniture a new lease of life with a quick lick of paint, the ideas over the next few pages are perfect for dipping your toes into a more colourful home.

Whenever I'm trying something new I like to test the waters slowly, and many of the colour converts I've spoken to over the years say they started out decorating with colour in this manner. In fact, as I travelled to style and shoot homes across Europe and America for this book with my photographer, Andrew Boyd, he would often text me in the days that followed our return to say that his wife was excited to try out the ideas we had shot together. At the start of the project their house was lacking in colour and by the end they had painted dining room chairs, changed their curtains and laid new white floors to help make their new colour addictions pop. So why not give these colour ideas a try? I have a feeling you'll be high on hue before you know it...

SCANDI BRIGHTS A series of painted dining chairs, colour-coordinated books and paste-coloured cushions bring a bright and friendly atmosphere to this Norwegian dining room.

TEN STEPS TO COLOUR CONFIDENCE

At times, decorating with colour can seem like a myriad of decisions and rules so daunting that we park it as a task that can only be tackled by expert interior decorators. Have you ever felt this way about bringing colour into your home? I promise you that this book will arm you with the knowledge to imprint your personality on your home by decorating successfully with colour. So before we explore the delights of colourful decorating, and how to get it right, let's take a look at ten quick and simple ways to feel more confident about decorating with hue.

★ **LEAVE YOUR FEAR AT THE FRONT DOOR** Decorating with colour is a rewarding activity that will result in a space that speaks directly to your inspirations and personality. Yes, you may make mistakes along the way, but it's amazing how much you can learn from them. Embrace the challenge and enjoy discovering a new relationship with colour.

★ **TAKE IT SLOWLY** Don't feel you need to decide on all your colours at once. Before you even decide on a space to decorate, it's best to take note of colours you are drawn towards. This way you can gradually build up an idea of your perfect palette so you're not creating a scheme 'blind' when you do start the decorating process. Knowing you already gravitate towards a hue in other areas of your life will make you feel more at ease when bringing it into a decorating scheme.

★ **TRUST YOUR INSTINCTS** Remember that colour is a very personal element of an interior; don't feel swayed by trends or a neighbour's home. Of course, these can be places to find ideas and inspiration, but don't feel tied to what is considered current – be free to adapt them to your own journey with colour.

★ **FIND A FOCUS** Perhaps you know the colours you like, but you're struggling with where to start? Pick a key piece for your scheme and use it as the reference point for the rest of the palette and room design. This could be anything from a rug to a smaller piece such as a vase or painting.

★ **PIN-POINT YOUR APPROACH** Once you've narrowed down the colours you like, it can help to decide how you plan on using them. Choosing to create a contrasting, tonal or harmonious palette upfront will help you pick the right shades and tones to introduce across the room.

FABULOUS FIREPLACE A striking combination of blue subway tiles and lime green walls creates a winning contrast that frames the woodburner in this upstate New York home. Flea market finds bring personal charm to the shelf above, while a disco ball and Pigeon lamp add a playful touch.

DELIGHTFULLY DOTTY
Ingrid Jansen uses colour and
pattern to create a cheerful vibe
in her Netherlands home. Homemade
textiles with eye-catching diamond
patterns, a whimsical lampshade and
painted multicoloured dots introduce
vibrancy to the neutral backdrop.

⭐ **BUILD ON YOUR EXISTING EXPERTISE**
While you may still be building your confidence with colourful decorating, you might be able to pull upon expertise from elsewhere? Perhaps you can throw together a perfect outfit in minutes or prepare a delicious meal without breaking sweat. Either way, look at how you pull colours together in other areas of your life and apply it to decorating – after all, the principles of which colours look good together are the same!

⭐ **PLAN, HUNT, GATHER** You're unlikely to go on holiday without taking time to research and gather information on the place you might like to visit. The same is true of decorating with colour: take time to pull together tear sheets, swatches and pictures so that you have a moodboard of ideas and inspirations to use as a springboard for your colour palette.

⭐ **SECTION THE SPACE** While it's important to keep in mind the whole room and how your chosen colours will sit within it, it will also help to tackle the space in sections. For example, start by layering colourful cushions and throws onto your sofa and live with the new hues before you introduce colour to other parts of the room. Living with the colours and seeing how they work will make you feel more confident when it comes to making bigger decorating decisions.

⭐ **START SMALL** As tempting as it might be to dive head first into a new kitchen or living room overhaul, it can help to start with a smaller room while you build your confidence with colour. Why not tackle your hallway, guest bathroom or a spare bedroom before taking on key rooms?

⭐ **LOOK FOR THE LIGHT** The light of a room has one of the biggest impacts on how your chosen colours will actually look in situ. In simple terms, with a north-facing room you'll be well placed with warm tones to balance the cooler light. In south-facing spaces using lighter shades will make the most of the abundance of light. Remember, you can layer in different shades of the same colour family into the scheme, so use this as a guide but don't feel too constrained.

BRASS BEAUTY Jonathan Adler marries tongue-in-cheek charm with opulent metallics as a foil to the teal and olive green upholstery of the Warren Platner chairs in his Shelter Island living room.

TURQUOISE TREAT (opposite)
The vibrant blue front door of this upstate New York home sets the tone for the saturated colours that grace the interior. Cheerfully filled flower pots serve as accent colours to the palette.

PASSIONATELY PURPLE
(right) Combining purple with a pillar box red creates an intense and passionate palette; painting the door surround in an accent colour serves to frame the entryway and creates drama.

CLASSIC COMBINATION
(below) The timeless palette of blue and white creates a cool coastal vibe to the front door of this Australian home, while statement numbers provide a graphic touch.

WILL'S COLOUR SECRET If you want to test the waters with a front door colour, try painting the door surround a cheerful bright tone before standing back to see how it looks. Then live with it for a few days before diving in and painting the whole door in a complementary or contrasting colour.

FRONT DOORS

FUN AND FABULOUS FIRST IMPRESSIONS

The age-old saying 'first impressions count' couldn't be truer when it comes to your home. From the postman to your best friend, anyone who visits will form an opinion on your space within minutes — so making a statement about you and your home should start before the door opens. Are you a fun and fearless city dweller who parties till dawn? Choose a playful bright to greet your guests, like sunflower yellow or a refreshing coral. If, however, you prefer to live a rural country dream, you may wish to opt for a calmer, more restrained hue, like olive green or petrol blue. Either way, be sure to make it anything but beige; after all, you want your home to be a reflection of you, not all the other houses on the street!

THREE IDEAS FOR A SENSATIONAL STAIRCASE

In any home the staircase is always a transitional area, a space to enjoy as you move between floors, presenting an ideal opportunity to have some fun with your design. Follow these ideas to create a knockout staircase that will wow you and your guests:

INTO THE BLUE (right) The owner of this Glasgow flat references her love for blue with names from the same colour family stickered onto the front of each staircase step.

STATEMENT STEPS (far right) Each step of this Swedish summerhouse staircase has been painted burnt orange to reflect the softer apricot hue of the tiles in the entryway below.

COOL CONTRAST (opposite) A painted glossy black banister is a striking contrast to the cool white stairs and walls in this Norwegian home. A pastel lilac chest offsets the tension between the black and white elements.

★ **SPINDLE SPECTRUM** A great way to create a colourful statement out of your staircase by only using a splash of colour is to paint the banister spindles in your favourite hue. You could take the look one step further by graduating the shade of each spindle to create an ombré effect. Or, for a graphic approach, painting just the banister alone in an eye-catching colour will command attention.

★ **TYPOGRAPHIC TOUCH** You can utilize the real estate of your staircase by stencilling numbers or words onto the face of each step. Whether you choose the different shades of your favourite colour or the lucky number of each family member you are guaranteed a stairway that becomes a talking point.

★ **A RUNNER-WAY SUCCESS** Even if you like to keep the floors in your home neutral throughout, stepping outside the box when it comes to the staircase can make your home soar in the style stakes. Try laying a multicoloured stripe runner along the centre of the stairs and it will make climbing each step a joy, never an effort.

SUPER STRIPES (this page)
The balcony doors in my bedroom
are quite narrow, so I chose to
dress the windows with a pair
of vertical striped linen curtains
that would emphasize their
height even when drawn open.

COOL CLASH (opposite, left)
I gave this everyday white chair
in my living room a bright update
by covering the seat cushion in
a graphic striped throw before
clashing it with a colourful
polka-dot cushion.

BLOOMIN' BEAUTIFUL
(opposite, centre) Vintage floral
wallpaper brings feminine charm
to this Swedish bedroom – the
rest of the space is fairly pared
back to allow the pattern to take
centre stage.

TACTILE TOUCH (opposite,
right) I believe bedroom décor
should play to the senses, so
I layered the master bedroom
of my London home with a jute
rug underfoot, a woollen topped
stool and linen curtains for a
totally tactile experience.

COLOUR, FABRIC AND PATTERN

If ever there was a fine example of how great things come in threes then this has to be it. Something magical happens when you combine colour, fabric and pattern. In fact, these three decorating elements are central to any scheme for many reasons. Firstly, the colour of a room sets the tone of the space, creating an energizing or calming atmosphere. Next, the fabric introduces texture into the mix – a tactile linen sofa cover evokes a feeling of breezy summer days, while a cashmere throw carries an air of sophistication and opulence. Finally, a touch of pattern can help bring depth to a scheme as it draws the eye towards or away from a specific part of the room. Of course, not every scheme calls for all three of these elements, but when used appropriately this trio can solve decorating dilemmas. Here are three ideas to try:

★ **VISUAL TRICKERY** Elongate the height of a room by hanging a pair of curtains with a vertical stripe pattern in the window – even if the window stops at waist height, draping the fabric to the floor will double the effect. Alternatively, a horizontal striped wallpaper can help fool the eye into thinking a room is wider than it actually is.

★ **RAISE THE ROOF** Painting a low ceiling in a complementary tone to the wall colour will soften the break between the point where the wall ends and the ceiling begins, making it feel higher.

★ **LIGHTEN THE SENSES** If you want to update an everyday white chair, why not wrap a colourful throw with a stripe detail around the seat pad? Then you can layer in a linen pillow with a polka dot pattern to throw the look off. As this is only a small part of a room it's okay to mix these two repeating patterns – ideal for adding life to a dull corner in a living room.

WILL'S COLOUR SECRET

If you are going to paint a piece of wooden furniture then a chalk-based paint will give the best finish and usually requires little preparation. However, if you use eggshell, be sure to clean the surface of grease and sand well before painting.

NEON ACCENT (this page) Hanging an acid yellow scarf from a red painted sideboard balances the bold colour and ties the piece into the art on the wall of this Netherlands home.

READING CORNER (opposite, top) A painted cabinet teamed with an Eames rocker and orange storage basket helps create a comfortable place to sit and read in this upstate New York home.

PAINT AND PAPER (opposite, bottom left) The wooden chest of drawers in this Norwegian home is given a quirky update by painting and papering alternate drawer fronts in tonal colours.

COLOUR UPDATE (opposite, bottom right) A quick lick of green paint refreshes a small reclaimed wooden stool, making it the perfect stage for a hot pink candle.

PAINTED FURNITURE

Bringing colour into your home doesn't have to mean expensive outlays or investments into brand-new furniture. For the price of a pot of paint and a few DIY supplies you can transform existing pieces in your home. A quick lick of paint can renew a tired piece of furniture into a star piece in the room, or it could take something unmemorable and make it unforgettable. A sideboard painted bright red will bring vibrancy to a living room or hallway, while a reclaimed wooden stool painted grass green and distressed with sandpaper creates an aged piece full of colourful character. Painting smaller pieces like these means you can be bold and brave with your colour choices. Why not try it? You could give your favourite room a whole new feel thanks to colour in a matter of hours.

A LIGHT TOUCH
(this page) Sometimes a subtle difference is all that is needed to create visual interest. In this Scandinavian dining room a wall-mounted cabinet is painted in a soft sky blue hue to define it against the white walls.

DISTRESSED DETAILS (opposite) The weathered finish on this painted green sideboard keeps the piece in line with the rustic industrial surroundings of the Copenhagen warehouse space.

MUSICAL CHAIRS
(this page) By alternating the upholstery and cushions on these Warren Platner chairs, the living area of this Shelter Island home takes on a lively and visually interesting feel.

ORANGE DELIGHT
(opposite, top) Placing four identical burnt orange chairs around a blackboard-topped round table makes a striking feature of the nook in this American kitchen.

PURPLE PUNCH
(opposite, below left) The owner of this upstate New York home uses a plain purple fabric armchair to anchor the multicoloured striped carpet. A striped cushion and arm covers tie the piece into the scheme.

THE BRIGHT SEAT
(opposite, below right) An occasional chair is painted true blue as a reference to the art hung on the wall in the living room of this Spanish farmhouse.

COLOURFUL CHAIRS

It wasn't until I started working on this book that I realized the significance of chairs in the home. From dining chairs and an office chair to a bedside table fashioned out of a spare chair and the multiple seating options in a living room, it became clear that they are integral to the design of each space. As soon as I thought about this I started to notice the multitude of ways you can use chairs to invite colour into a room. Whether you decide to pepper a series of different coloured wooden chairs around a dining table or reupholster some retro finds from a flea market, it's worthwhile considering chairs to be the lead in your colour scheme. Occasional chairs present an opportunity to introduce an offbeat hue into an otherwise coordinated living room scheme, while a number of repeated chairs in a single hue will create a focal point when placed around a dining table.

Colour **IDEAS**

Painted dining chairs anchor this white table and make it the statement feature of the space

DINING DELIGHTS
Placing colourfully painted dining chairs around the white table helps to make the dining area a focal point in the open-plan, all-white space of this Scandinavian home.

FOUR WAYS TO ROCK STATEMENT LIGHTING

Another really simple way to add wow to a room is to introduce a colourful light fitting. It can be a pendant, wall sconce, floor lamp or table light — the key is to make it the star of the room with an eye-catching colour. The décor of a room evolves over time and it's important to consider how your lighting options sit in a new scheme. It's not just about buying new, but also about updating existing lighting pieces to work in the new colour scheme. Why not refresh a metal lamp by spray-painting it a new colour? Or, if you are redecorating other elements of the space, you could craft a lampshade in corresponding fabric to refashion an existing floor or table lamp for the updated look. Whatever route you take, if you lavish your lights with colour you will be on the right path to brilliant brights!

★ **ARTFUL ANGLEPOISE** The trusted Anglepoise lamp is not only a practical task lamp, but its shape and form are equally as impressive. You can use colour to emphasize the striking design of this table light by opting for a sleek, matt finish blue hue.

★ **REALLY RETRO** Do you like to introduce a throw-back element to your decorating schemes? If so, a mid-century modern mushroom lamp brings a charming touch of retro to a space. If you choose a shade from the same family as the wall colour then you will help the beautiful curves of the design shine.

★ **PENDANT POP** I think all-white rooms are always crying out for a hit of colour, but it doesn't have to be much. A stand-alone Perspex pendant shade in the centre of the room is all that is needed to create a statement lighting feature.

★ **METALLIC MAGIC** Choosing a metallic finish for a lampshade is the perfect choice for a room that's already commanded by a strong colour statement. The reflective nature of the metallic will help bounce light around the room and give the space an air of luxury.

FORM AND FUNCTION A blue Anglepoise lamp brings both style and practicality to the sideboard of this weekend home in upstate New York.

COLOURFULLY CURVED The mid-century modern mushroom lamp adds retro curves and detail to this American home office packed full of flea-market finds.

HANG OUT This all-white living room in the Netherlands is graced with a playful pink Perspex pendant that becomes a statement colour pop in the otherwise neutral space.

SHIMMERING SILVER Choosing a metallic lampshade for this bedside table lamp invites a little glamour into the master bedroom of this Netherlands home.

COLOUR COCKTAILS

My home is full of colourful and whimsical vignettes

MIXING YOUR SIGNATURE PALETTE

Your favourite cuisine, drink, record, outfit and so on are all a reflection of who you are and how you like to live your life. By the same token, the colours you pick for your home are imprinting your personality onto what can feel like an overwhelmingly blank canvas. However, I believe that decorating a home should always be an enjoyable process; something you look forward to, just like cocktail hour at the end of a long working week! When you sit down in a bar and you're faced with four pages of cocktails, you'll probably turn to the bar staff for advice on what to pick. No doubt you feel the same when you visit a hardware store and you're faced with a paint card that offers hundreds of different colours shown in an array of tints, tones and shades.

With that in mind, this chapter is designed to help you find the colours that speak to you; to show you how to turn colour inspiration into a meaningful decorating scheme and to give advice on how to mix hues together to varying degrees of strength. Just like real drinks, these colour cocktails are versatile enough to be mixed to personal décor taste. Whether you like your decorating schemes as vivacious and strong as your favourite tipple, or prefer to take a gentler approach, this collection of palettes will show you multiple ways to mix a colour cocktail so that it will become your signature palette.

Flowers are a great way to try out a new palette; you can always take inspiration from your favourite vases or a piece of artwork, too. If you like the blooms, you could consider extending the colours across the rest of the scheme.

COLOURFUL COLLECTION
I use this sideboard in the living room of my London home as a place to display an ever-evolving mix of vases, prints, books and fresh blooms.

FINDING INSPIRATION

The best way to discover colours that speak to you is by focusing on those you are naturally drawn towards; you'll already be making colour-based decisions without consciously realizing that you're gravitating towards certain hues over others. A great way to start cataloguing your inspiration is to look through the pictures you took on a recent holiday, or even quick snaps from a weekend walk. Gather together your favourites and see if you can spot any colour themes running through the shortlist. With your photographs chosen, turn your attention to magazines and retail catalogues to pull together a moodboard of tear sheets and fabrics that match the hues in the photographs. Be instinctive in your approach to the task; don't overthink your choices or include tear sheets unless they genuinely inspire you. If you do this, you'll soon see how your moodboard represents a colour palette personal to you. You'll see over the coming pages that this is exactly how I develop my own colour palettes: each of the colour cocktails starts with my own inspiration pictures, personal experiences and memories of colour for the given palette; the moodboard I pulled together to create a decorating plan for each colour scheme follows; and, finally, real-life homes from all over the world, including my own, show how these knockout palettes have been used to create colourfully stylish rooms that pack a serious punch of personality.

BOUGAINVILLEA BRIGHTS The vibrant hot pink hue of a pretty bougainvillea plant that climbed the side of this Spanish building is an example of how the colours in my travel photographs inspire my palettes back home.

All of the colour cocktail palletes were inspired
by my own travel photographs — just like this
picture of a vibrant pink bougainvillea in
Spain, which inspired me so much that
I framed it to use in my master bedroom!

Sunshine lemon
AND
SALMON PINK

THE CANDY CRUSH

BALEARIC BEAUTIES

In the summer of 2012 I travelled to the Balearic Islands in search of colour inspiration. Disconnecting from my laptop and mobile for ten days, I was armed with only my camera as I wandered the cobbled streets of the traditional Spanish towns. Feeling at my most relaxed for several years, I enjoyed taking in the mix of sun-soaked pastels and saturated bright façades of the painted buildings. As I travelled from town to town I started to see a pattern emerging: many of my photographs featured yellow and pink buildings stood side by side. I felt drawn to the energizing combination of these two complementary hues; the cheerful optimism of the yellow was tempered beautifully by the romantic softness of the pink. I knew on my return I needed to explore the combination further, and so my love for The Candy Crush began.

COLOUR
WILL'S
SECRET

Don't be deterred if you don't find the right shade first time as even top designers will try out multiple testers on the wall before settling on their final choice. Paint a few samples side by side and then live with them for a few days to see how they look at different times of the day.

SPANISH SPLASH
The Mediterranean is full of colour inspiration, and nowhere more so than Spain's Balearic Islands, which are awash with colour. I took a picture of these two crumbling, character-packed façades in Mahon, the capital of Menorca. I love the irony in how these clearly aged buildings take on an almost youthful feel thanks to their colourful nature.

COLOUR AND TEXTURE ARE BEST FRIENDS

I decided to decorate with The Candy Crush palette in my snug because it offered a palette that was cheerful and uplifting with a retained element of calm. Distressing my painted furniture to create weathered textures brought an aged feel to the colour scheme, and gave an edge to the otherwise saccharine palette. That's the wonderful nature of colour – you can alter the look of a palette by pairing it with another decorating element, such as texture. It's this juxtaposition between the lemon and carnation colour palette and the rough texture of the statement cabinet that tells the story of the space. In fact, I decided to introduce these worn textures to the scheme as a direct result of the picture I took of the two weathered pink and yellow buildings in Spain (previous page).

The Candy CRUSH MOODBOARD

This versatile colour palette can be mixed to differing strengths: use pastel shades for a saccharine-sweet scheme or choose chalky, duller shades paired with weathered textures for a more mature look.

Painting the inside of my bookcase white provided a neutral base to layer in the yellow and pink hues of The Candy Crush palette; one of my framed prints propped on top of the unit and a hanging Edison bulb fill 'dead' space in the room.

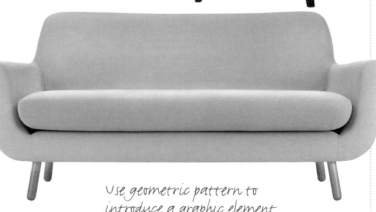

Use geometric pattern to introduce a graphic element to this delicate palette.

FABULOUS FELT The candy-coloured felt seat pads in this Shelter Island home show how colour can be used to visually fuse together individual elements of an open-plan space.

TWO WAYS TO MIX THE CANDY CRUSH

2

★ **SUGARY SWEET** Whichever way you wish to mix this palette, whether it's adding a fresh and sugary sweet feeling to a playful kitchen or breathing life into a sophisticated living room, it will always bring a sense of youthful energy to a space. Anki Zilverblauw achieved the former look in the kitchen of her Netherlands home (right) by mixing The Candy Crush using a soft pastel pink accented with a shot of canary yellow. This arresting scheme is achieved by using pink shades across the fundamental elements of the room, such as the fridge, while layers of glossy yellow accents inject vibrancy into the dominant pastels in the palette.

★ **CONFIDENT CONTRAST** Alternatively you can use The Candy Crush to inject colour into a refined living space. Pink and yellow felted seat pads around the floating fireplace in Jonathan Adler and Simon Doonan's Shelter Island home punctuate the concrete feature with their bonbon-like hues. Whereas The Candy Crush colour palette can be used to make a confident statement (as you can see in the Amsterdam kitchen overleaf), Jonathan and Simon's open-plan living area is an example of when colour takes a supporting role to an existing focal point. The floating fireplace is such a striking architectural feature that these small additions of colour are used to emphasize the shape and form of the curved centrepiece in the space. The result of swapping out the glossy pastel finishes that dominated the first look for more refined, tactile felt textiles is a more sophisticated scheme – lifted by a dash of Jonathan's renowned playfulness, thanks to an idiosyncratic vase full of cerise pink peonies.

PASTEL PRETTY The kitchen space of this Netherlands home is a story of contrasts, where an industrial wood burner is paired with a pastel palette across the pink fridge and glossy yellow step stool. Wallpaper emphasizes the shape of the flue, drawing the eye upwards and creating a spacious feel.

PINK PUNCH (left) The light-flooded kitchen of an Amsterdam artist shows a saturated take on The Candy Crush colour palette, which is tempered by the additional contrasts seen between the pairing of a vintage dining table and an easel displaying artwork against sleek modern cabinetry.

BRIGHT BREW (below) An eclectic mix of tea tins in cheerful colours and pretty patterns make the most of the open storage in this Dutch kitchen. A saffron keepsake box, spring green serving tray and bright red teapot are colourful accents to the glossy pink walls.

THE CANDY CRUSH CONCENTRATED

Artist Mariska Meijiers is far from colour shy: her paintings and textiles are a riot of bright, intoxicating hues – and her home follows the lead of her works. The kitchen of Mariska's Amsterdam apartment concentrates the core pink and yellow palette of The Candy Crush cocktail to create an intensely colourful scheme. Hot pink walls in a gloss finish wrap around the entire kitchen, creating a pool of colour that sections the cooking area from the rest of the open-plan space. Sleek modern units contrast with an antique table that is anchored by an ochre animal-hide rug. Splashes of saffron and golden yellow accessories are layered across the kitchen, while cerise pink seat pads upon the Eames chairs nod to the statement walls. The success of intensifying The Candy Crush palette lies in the lack of pattern across the fundamental elements of the space. Introducing two strong shades side by side in this manner means the scheme requires a sense of simplicity to give those hues breathing space. By keeping pattern to a minimum, Mariska's concentrated take on The Candy Crush palette not only reflects her vivacious and spirited personality, but also proves that going double on your colour palette can work wonders.

HOT SEAT (opposite) The cerise pink seat pads on the Eames chairs around the dining table in this Amsterdam apartment are a bold accent to the rug underneath.

COLOUR WILL'S SECRET

A rich shade of pink is the perfect statement hue to bring warmth to a light and airy space because it has more mellow qualities compared to red, even when used liberally.

THE LIME DIVINE

THE JOY OF COLOUR WATCHING . . .

Many people say that one of their favourite pastimes is sitting in a café, fresh coffee in hand and nothing but an hour of people watching stretched out ahead of them. I like to do things a little differently: I don't people watch, I colour watch! If you find me on a park bench or sat on a train, the chances are I'll be searching out ideas and inspiration for a new colour palette. This was true when I sat at a tiny roadside café in France last year; and I didn't have to look too far before the idea for The Lime Divine came to me. It was like any other quintessential continental café scene in Europe, where small round tables and folding chairs were jumbled by the road, casually wrapped around the front of the building. Although each set of table and chairs was a mix of different colours, it was the lime and azure blue pairing that really caught the attention of my colour-loving eye. It's often telling when a pairing of hues stands out among a sea of colours; remember the palette doesn't change so if it works 'out in the field' it can work back at home, too. So next time you're at a café, look around you, because you might just discover a new palette . . .

WILL'S SECRET

If you're unsure about a palette, why not start small before investing too heavily in the scheme? Find a coloured vase in your chosen hue (or paint an existing one) and fill it with a bunch of blooms in the other colour. Live with it for a few days, and if you still like it you will feel confident about introducing the new palette elsewhere in the space.

PERFECT PAIR A chance pairing of two green and blue folding chairs I spotted outside a café in France sparked the inspiration for The Lime Divine palette.

zesty hues!

WILL'S COLOUR INSPIRATION

B
B

CAFE
BRIGHTS

HIGH ON LIME The floor-to-ceiling lime walls in this upstate New York living room bring punch to the flea-market finds and weathered furniture layered throughout the scheme. The vivid turquoise throw draped on the sofa creates depth and interest.

The Lime DIVINE

MOODBOARD

The key to success with this palette is to take one of two routes: you can lavish key pieces with colour such as walls and floors and keep furniture and accessories neutral. Or, switch it up and use layers of lime and turquoise shades to add interest to a neutral space.

Treat cabinet tops like mini stages to display all your wares. Raina Kattleson's storage unit allows a statement lamp to hold court alongside flea-market finds.

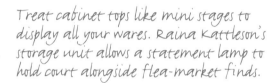

Try dipping your toes into this vibrant palette with one statement piece, like a sofa or floor lamp.

ECLECTIC DINING Raina Kattleson creates a lived-in vibe for her open-plan dining room, with a bookcase full of found accessories, vases and books. A Moooi pendant lamp and green painted bentwood chairs anchor the table and zone it as the dining area.

MAKING EVERYTHING WORK IN AN OPEN-PLAN SPACE

Colour is a great decorating element to help zone an open-plan space. because it provides a visual indicator to the change of purpose in the various parts of the room. The continuation of lime green across the walls in this open-plan living space ties all the sections together and offers a synergy between each area. Meanwhile, an array of blues are layered into the space to signify the zones: an ultramarine painted cabinet and tiled fireplace draw the eye along the feature wall of the room, making statements out of both in the process. The change in pace to a steel-blue denim colour for the rug and radiator pulls the far end of the space together, grouping the living room furniture. Surprise orange accents complete the scheme by inviting visual interest and echoing the clean finish of the lime walls.

HOW TO MIX THE LIME DIVINE

There's a fresh, healthy and energizing feel to this colour duo; the lime brings a zesty kick that's tempered by the azure blue hues. In fact, The Lime Divine is evidence that it can work to bring two strong colours together, as their joint intensity actually serves to bring balance to the palette. Raina Kattleson's open-plan living space in her upstate New York home demonstrates this balance perfectly. The smooth lime green base throughout serves as the perfect backdrop to layer in small splashes of blue hues throughout the space. By letting one of the two main colours take the lead, it allows the other to be used as a tool to break up the strength of the dominant hue. In the dining area a bookcase styled with an eclectic mix of blue vases and books provides the accent pieces needed to calm the lively lime walls. Introducing colour-blocked bentwood chairs in a deeper shade of chartreuse green around the dining table anchors it as a key piece in the space. Meanwhile, a Moooi pendant creates a feeling of intimacy at the dining table without competing with the statement walls.

SIDE-TABLE DISPLAY
A turquoise vase perfectly offsets the lime green wall of this American living room. Mixing rough and smooth finishes creates visual interest.

COLOURFUL COSY The open-plan living space in this American home sees a palette of bold green and blue hues paired with lashings of inviting textiles to create a vibrant yet welcoming vibe.

Use colour to section an open-plan space.

FIVE STEPS
TO TAKE THE LIME DIVINE UP A LEVEL

MIAMI BRIGHTS

Beth Arrowood's Miami home is like a tropical treat of colourful decorating, as she has taken The Lime Divine palette to the next level. As the founder of Miami-based NIBA rugs, it's no surprise that Beth has used a bold patterned rug as the basis of her sunroom. Beth believes one should always start decorating a room with the rug and work up from there, and her home is testament to this being sound advice. This robust take on such a bold scheme is successful because the fundamental elements of the space, the rug, textiles, furniture and so on, all call upon the red thread that runs throughout – the turquoise and lime palette.

★ **FLOOR COVERING** The floor space is the main surface area of the room, so utilize it by covering it with an oversized rug. Make a striking statement by choosing a design that marries the key colours with a visually interesting pattern.

★ **TEXTILES** Adding additional colour to a space through textiles helps to make the colour statement more observable, while simultaneously creating a soft, cosy feel. Opt for full-length drapes to take advantage of the opportunity to add a block of colour to the space.

★ **PATTERN** Introducing a bold and repetitive pattern will help you create a more flamboyant scheme. Be sure to match the pattern to the fundamental colours of the space – lime and turquoise – as this will result in a coherent final look.

★ **FURNITURE** The central elements of any room are almost always the furniture, so use the individual pieces to bring further vibrancy to the scheme. In this case, you're looking to up the colour ante, so opt for a sofa in the opposite hue to the walls or textiles behind it. This juxtaposition of hues is an easy way to create a wow factor in the room.

★ **REPETITION** When you combine such strong shades with graphic pattern, it's important to use repetition as a tool to anchor all the elements of the space. Consider placing identical side tables and lamps either side of the sofa, or echo the fabric used in the drapes in cushions.

PATTERN FANTASTIC In this Miami sunroom the graphic Greek key pattern of the curtains and the floral detail in the rug achieve synergy thanks to their lime green shades.

WILL'S COLOUR SECRET To successfully combine strong colour and bold pattern, it's important to stick to using block colours in corresponding hues to their patterned counterparts. This will help you to create a harmonious scheme that consists of strong individual elements that work together and don't compete with one another visually in the space.

Cardinal Red AND GREEK BLUE

THE STRAWBERRY SPLIT

DATE YOUR PALETTE BEFORE YOU MARRY IT

My colour-loving eye rarely rests from its hunt for a new palette idea, and while some colour combinations win my affections from the moment I see them, other pairings develop over time. I often compare this to the dating period of a new relationship: this is the time where I can canvas my potential new palette and discover which parts of its personality work for me. This was true of the red and blue palette that makes up The Strawberry Split, the idea for which began at a farmer's market early one summer. With the strawberry season in full swing many of the stalls were awash with a sea of red berries, their intense hue cooled only by Greek blue flashes in the rims of their punnets. The duo certainly stood out amongst the mass of other colours on display, but I was keen to seek out other ideas to marry the two hues. A few months later I was in France when I happened upon a crimson red fire hydrant in front of a richly painted blue wall – the colour was so inviting I wanted to swim in it. I recalled the memory of the strawberry punnets at the farmer's market and thought how the duo worked well when the blue half of the palette took centre stage. I had discovered that in this colour relationship the blue shade wears the trousers, but that it wouldn't be half as tempting without its red counterpart to complete the pairing. A day or so later I walked past a pair of red and blue painted shopfronts in London's Covent Garden. I knew I was ready to invite The Strawberry Split home …

COLOUR WILL'S SECRET

When you are planning a colour scheme try placing inspiration pictures and magazine tear sheets from various scenarios together. This can help focus a colour palette idea into a vision that will work in your own home.

PALETTE ADDICT
This vibrant fire hydrant in France was perfectly framed by the wash of blue on the wall behind it. Seeing colourful shopfronts and punnets of fruit at a farmer's market in London all led me to create The Strawberry Split palette.

I like to think of the blues in this palette as the calming counterparts to their commanding red partners, so use blues across hero pieces and pepper red accents in around them.

A graphic chevron pattern adds fuel to the fire of this tomato red colour and will give it more emphasis in the scheme.

A duo of vintage red and blue clocks are ideal accessories to offtset the floral wallpaper in the bedroom of this swedish summerhouse.

COLOUR POP This brightly painted wardrobe I found at a flea market brings a shot of colour to my London home. A vintage flag hung down one side brings graphic punch, and vintage accessories grouped together on the top of the piece introduce the cardinal red accents that make this colourful corner sing.

THREE STEPS TO STYLE A VIBRANT VIGNETTE

★ **HEIGHT** The key to making a group of objects work when placed together is to vary the height of each piece in order to create depth. Arrange the pieces in a jumbled version rather than high to low, as this will give a more natural look to the collection.

★ **COLOUR** The main purpose of this vignette is to introduce accent pieces to the room's statement piece of furniture, the colour of which is referenced by the splash of blue in a mini print that pulls the two elements together. The darkened cardinal red shades temper the brightness of the blue cabinet, while the surprise introduction of yellow adds freshness to the palette.

★ **TEXTURE** To bring visual interest to the vignette it's important to switch up the textures used in different pieces. Here I used a bold typographic print to give a graphic feel, which I then carried through the vignette with the petrol can. The weathered and embossed nature of the type on the petrol can allows the second introduction of a type-centric piece to sit comfortably in the scheme without competing with the typographic print.

A glass jar bursting with freshly cut daisies softens the rustic feel of this colourful collection in my home.

HOW TO INTENSIFY THE STRAWBERRY SPLIT

While my painted blue cabinet and vintage red accessories are a great way to mix The Strawberry Split and bring colour to an empty corner in an all-white rented apartment, this palette also works well when it's projected across a whole scheme. The master bedroom in Raina Kattleson's upstate New York home keeps blue at the core of the colour palette, but extends its reach from a statement piece of furniture to cover the walls. The result is a rich and intense Greek blue base that wraps around all sides of the room. Although dramatic, the space still feels cocooning and calming thanks to the tranquil and peaceful nature of blue – perfect for a bedroom.

When using a single colour this extensively in a scheme it's important to introduce a second colour to balance the palette. Raina's take on The Strawberry Split was to layer a series of red shades into the scheme by dressing the bed with vibrant textiles. A Mexican Suzani bedspread in an orange-red, vermilion hue helps to pull the eye through the space and across the bed. Layers of cushions and pillows in a mix of cardinal and crimson coloured prints are further pronounced because of the exotic blue walls behind. As Raina has introduced multiple shades of red in the bedding textiles, they become the secondary colour in the scheme, which is why a third introduction of colour, in the form of a magenta pink throw, is an ideal accent to complete the scheme and gently soften the intensity of the all over red and blue palette.

WILL'S COLOUR SECRET

Look at the light in your room before you pick your desired shade of blue to paint on the walls – if it's a bright space then it will suit a cool blue that reflects the light, whereas in darker corners you can use deeper, more dramatic shades of blue that will evoke a warmer and cosier feel.

EXOTIC DREAMS

A generous lick of Greek blue paint on the walls paired with a Mexican Suzani bedspread gives this master bedroom an exotic feel. A delicate white paper fan tempers the intensity of the blue, while red accessories and art pull the red shades through the scheme.

THE MINT BLISS

FALLING FOR MINT IN THE CITY OF LIGHT

Given that it's famed for being the most romantic city in the world, you would be forgiven for skirting Paris when choosing a destination for colour inspiration. As I walked up the 284 steps of the Arc de Triomphe my mind was racing with excitement, not for the colours I hoped to see, but in anticipation of the breathtaking views I expected to be greeted with at the summit. I hadn't been wrong – the views from the top were just as beautiful as I had been told. Yet amongst all the grandeur of the city below there was a lone hue that caught my eye. As I clicked the lens of my camera I stopped, just like a magpie would at the sight of something shiny, as the weathered verdigris copper rooftops in the distance came into focus. I was thrilled to feel so inspired by colour at such an unexpected moment, and, as a self-confessed colour addict, it made the experience all the more special.

Back on solid ground, I turned to walk off the tree-lined avenues and down a back street to find a tucked-away restaurant for lunch. As I crossed the road I saw what looked like a stream of mint-coloured water, which on closer inspection was the rust from a series of copper pipes above. I later discovered that the rust would have taken more than 25 years to take on its mint appearance and I marvelled at the thought of a colour developing naturally over an extended period of time. It was exciting to see an unexpected colour story developing just minutes after first seeing the mint Parisian rooftops. Having been stopped in my tracks twice by the same hue, I could feel I my colour-loving heart falling for the soft and gentle shade of green. So with my inspiration pictures snapped and mint firmly on the mind, I headed to lunch to moodboard my latest colour cocktail – The Mint Bliss.

CITY OF MINT Looking over Parisian rooftops from the top of the Arc de Triomphe led me to discover the minted copper rooftops of the city that inspired me to create The Mint Bliss colour cocktail.

It all started with mint rooftops in Paris . . .

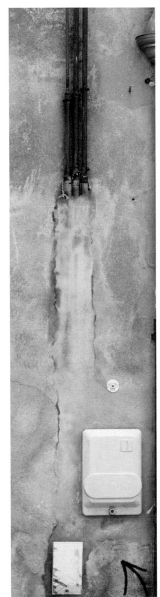

My palette ideas are sometimes sparked in unusual places: I love that you never know when colour inspiration will strike!

TEXTURED CHARM
The office in my London apartment is a riot of colour and texture, with a weathered mint desk and distressed yellow Tolix-style chair at the heart of the scheme. A Mexican pink handle brings a surprise dash of hue to the palette.

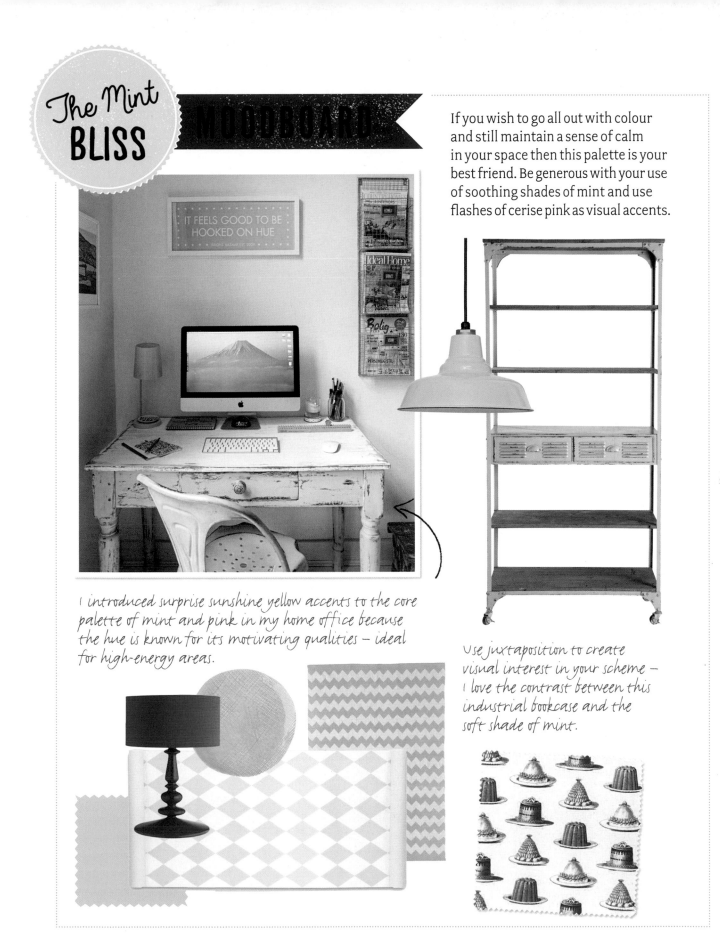

The Mint BLISS

MOODBOARD

If you wish to go all out with colour and still maintain a sense of calm in your space then this palette is your best friend. Be generous with your use of soothing shades of mint and use flashes of cerise pink as visual accents.

IT FEELS GOOD TO BE HOOKED ON HUE

I introduced surprise sunshine yellow accents to the core palette of mint and pink in my home office because the hue is known for its motivating qualities – ideal for high-energy areas.

Use juxtaposition to create visual interest in your scheme – I love the contrast between this industrial bookcase and the soft shade of mint.

RIGHT REFLECTION (left)
A hanging mirror helps diffuse light around this pretty guest bedroom, encouraging it to fall into a darker corner of the room.

PERFECT PISTACHIO (right)
The soft and subtle shade of green painted on the wood-panelled walls of the bedroom in this Swedish summerhouse creates a colourful canvas for the vintage furniture, delicate textiles and farmhouse accessories in the room.

WHY IT PAYS TO MAXIMIZE WITH MINT

Feature walls are often used to create a statement in colourful interiors as there is a common misconception that you shouldn't paint all the walls of a room in the same colour. Ironically, if you maximize the use of a single hue across all the walls of a room it can pay dividends to the rest of the features in the space. The key is to decorate all over with a single pastel shade, like mint, as the result will be a colourful yet unassuming backdrop for the other elements of the space.

The Swedish summerhouse of resident Gothenburg designer Elisabeth Dunker is a case in point. With friends and family keen to escape the heat of the city to stay at the Dunkers' summerhouse, Elisabeth set about increasing space for guests by converting an old hen house at the end of the garden into a spare bedroom. As part of the transformation from weathered outbuilding to a tranquil bedroom, Elisabeth painted all of the wood-panelled walls in a refreshing shade of mint. Soft and subtle pastel shades, such as mint, sea foam and pistachio, are perfect for rooms that call for a generous dose of colour that won't subjugate the space. In fact, shades of sea foam are often so subtle that they will help to emphasize the existing character of the space. In Elisabeth's guest bedroom the mint colouring exaggerates the horizontal lines of the wood panelling, which visually elongates the room in the process. And despite all the walls being mint in the bedroom, the hue's mild properties encourage the other features of the room to stay at the forefront of the scheme. The natural light reflected from the delicate pastel walls helps draw focus to the wooden floorboards and vintage bed. For best results, introduce your accent colours sparingly – splashes of rose pink pair well with chalky greens, but you could also double up with multiple shades of one colour to create a tonal scheme.

WILL'S COLOUR SECRET

Tonal schemes use one colour, but in several different tones. To create a coordinated and harmonized scheme, decorate with the key colour across the fundamental elements of the room (walls, ceiling, furniture), and then use accessories and accent pieces to layer in darker or lighter tints that originate from it.

Liquorice
AND
VERMILION

THE TANGERINE DREAM

BRIGHT LIGHTS, BIG CITY

Like any major metropolitan location, New York City is a melting pot of creativity, and with that comes an abundance of colour inspiration. While the city's street art and eye-catching fashions provide daily fodder for palette ideas, sometimes it's the natural events that surround all of these elements that actually spark the inspiration for a colour scheme.

During a visit to Manhattan in April 2013, the city was experiencing a heat wave that brought with it soaring temperatures and blue skies foreign to the usual damp, grey weather of the early spring season. One afternoon I was downtown, having spent a large part of the day attending meetings in corporate office rooms; needless to say I had more than reached saturation point of strip lighting, beige walls and artificial air. I remember the moment I stepped out onto the sidewalk from the cold, overly marbled and unmemorable lobby of the building. Walking down one of the island's linear avenues, I was immediately struck by the rich golden hour light. The sun's evening rays shimmered across the glass windows of the warehouse buildings, projecting its golden, honey-hued light proudly yet softly down the street, creating inky, black silhouettes of everything in its path. I felt inspired by how the richness of the sun's rays intensified from scorching white at the centre to rich amber, all the way to intense shades of orange and vermilion at each ray's end. Despite the mass of concrete, high-rise buildings and continued sirens, the walk back to my hotel felt almost ethereal and dream like. Back at my hotel and looking out of the window from the 27th floor, I marvelled at how the light created a contrast between its rich orange colouring against the warehouse buildings and the jet-black shadows it created behind. That night, kept awake with jet lag, I mulled over the experience: I knew I had to see how this contrast would look in an interior, and so I devised The Tangerine Dream palette.

RAY OF LIGHT
The rich shades of orange from the sun's rays against the inky black shadows and silhouettes created during the golden hour in Manhattan were the catalyst for The Tangerine Dream colour cocktail.

THE GOLDEN HOUR, NYC

WILL'S COLOUR INSPIRATION
B B
SUNSET HUES

MOODBOARD

Be brave! The best way to wow with this palette is to embrace a dark base and then use tangerine orange to make a hero out of one or two key elements in the scheme.

A lacquered orange front door sets the effervescent tone that bubbles throughout Jonathan Adler and Simon Doonan's 60s inspired Shelter Island vacation house – a pleasing juxtaposition to the austere modernist black façade of the building.

Strong colours such as these can take strong pattern – but introduce it in small doses for best results. Try a throw, pillow or lampshade, for example.

COLOUR PLAY A tomato red chimney is testament to Jonathan Adler's 'Happy Chic' design philosophy — start with a classic foundation and then add a splash of humour and idiosyncrasy, and a healthy dose of chic.

THREE STEPS
TO MAKE BOLD BEDROOM COLOURS A SUCCESS

Don't shy away from decorating with bold brights in the bedroom — follow these steps to create a palette that commands attention without jeopardizing serenity.

⭐ **DELICIOUS DARKS** Darker tones are ideal for bold bedroom palettes, because they offer an element of drama and surprise while concurrently being cosy and cocooning; use these shades as a base to anchor the statement bright.

⭐ **BRILLIANT BRIGHTS** Introduce a single bright to accent the darker base palette and it will bring a touch of energy and vibrancy to the scheme without overpowering the space.

⭐ **NULLIFYING NEUTRALS** Complete the palette by foiling the dark and bright combination with a series of calming neutral shades and textures, such as burlap, jute, whitewashed wood panelling, stone and mohair.

MATERIAL MIX (right)
The master bedroom of this Shelter Island property juxtaposes rough and smooth to create a tactile environment — tiling sits alongside feathers; burlap alongside metal.

BEDSIDE BEAUTIES (left)
A bunch of cerise pink peonies encourage a bright and positive awakening when placed beside the bed.

PUNCTUATE WITH COLOUR

Sometimes a colour statement can be made by introducing a single burst of bright into an otherwise muted palette. The striking contrast of hues in the master bedroom of Jonathan Alder and Simon Doonan's Shelter Island modernist beach house uses this method to encourage a focal point for the eye. They key to the scheme's success lies in the simplicity of the palette – a single hit of tangerine from the Cameroonian juju headdress punctuates the slate-grey glaze of the tiled wall behind. Although arresting, this combination of colours creates a graphic and contemporary design that doesn't detract from the layers of detail and texture, as seen in the bedding textiles and Adler's personally designed tiling.

THE CERULEAN SPLASH

SWIMMING IN THE SIMPLICITY OF SEASIDE SHADES

Life by the sea has a distinct draw to it, don't you think? There's something incredibly appeasing about the rhythmic lapping of waves against the shore, the salty sea air blowing through your hair as you saunter through the sand. I often feel at my calmest when I'm near the sea and will happily walk for hours to find little-known coves and beaches whenever I'm lucky enough to find myself at the coast. Perhaps it's the simplicity of the natural elements that frees up the mind to let memories and colour inspiration stick; the refreshingly rudimentary trio of sun, sand and sea is a far cry from the hectic buzz of city life where a thousand sensory experiences perpetually shout for your attention. While urban dwellings bear colour inspiration of their own kind, I find that the very simplicity of coastal elements encourages me to notice the colour details in the everyday. I believe this is true for others, too, as I so often see buildings in seaside towns that reflect their coastal surroundings with their saturated yet weathered blue and yellow façades. The sky-blue and school-bus-yellow palette of this coastal building in the South of France felt like a pronounced nod to natural maritime elements of the area. Just like the sunshine yellow boat that was tethered to an aged wooden jetty as it bobbed up and down in the cerulean water of the harbour, the doors of this building had distressed, sun-warped wooden planks with flaking paint and rusted iron brackets. I had discovered a colour palette that looked good enough to swim in. Its name? The Cerulean Splash.

COASTAL CHARM
The weathered façade of this French building reflects the colours and textures of its coastal location with a striking primary palette of saturated sunshine yellow and aged sky blue.

The Cerulean SPLASH

MOODBOARD

For me, this is the ultimate summertime palette; inspired by the coast and reflecting the ocean, it is at once colourful and calm. Mix old with new and embrace an array of blues to create a standout scheme.

Give an aged look to your chosen blues by mixing with white to achieve a weathered effect.

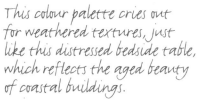

This colour palette cries out for weathered textures, just like this distressed bedside table, which reflects the aged beauty of coastal buildings.

FARMHOUSE DINING (opposite) Jonquil yellow painted dining chairs, a distressed wooden table, painted blue doors and a chandelier handmade from iron with blue beading detail lend homespun, rustic charm to the dining area of Javier Requejo's Spanish farmhouse.

★ **PLAYFUL MODERN** You can be sure your scheme will carry plenty of visual bang if it's centred around a colour-block theme. The look is ideal for a family home because it gives a room a cheerful and youthful feel. Recreate the look by ensuring all the fundamental elements of the space are a single block of either yellow or blue. Foil these brights with a cool white background, as this will really make the individual elements of the scheme zing.

CHEERFUL COLOUR (this page) Anki Zilverblauw uses Bondi blue curtains, a mustard yellow sideboard and a sky blue Eames rocker as bold colour blocks.

HOMESPUN HEROES (opposite, left) Handmade pieces, found accessories and a knitted throw are the colour heroes here.

ARTFUL DESTRUCTION (opposite, right) The contrast between the chic black walls and striking blue and yellow artwork creates a dramatic and arresting vibe.

THREE WAYS TO MIX THE CERULEAN SPLASH

This versatile colour palette can be mixed in order to match your surroundings. Whether you're looking to complement the rustic textures of a farmhouse or add zing to a modern space, this duo of hues always delivers.

★ **COUNTRY RUSTIC** A calming, comfortable and charming vibe is central to this look, so before you add brighter hues begin with a neutral base made up of soft white sofas and pale sky blue walls; adding a dark hide rug will ground these lighter, floaty shades of the space. Next, introduce the Cerulean Splash colours with yellow blooms from the garden to give a homespun feel.

★ **STRIKING CONTEMPORARY** Perhaps you live in a city apartment like artist Mariska Meijers's Amsterdam home? If so, this arresting take on The Cerulean Splash could be for you. Enveloping noir-painted walls create an intense and dramatic atmosphere that juxtaposes to stunning effect with the fresh and jaunty yellow and blue hues in the artwork; the deconstructed nature of the piece gives this contrast further prominence. The key to this look is to ensure you pair the refreshing hues of the Cerulean Splash palette with an intensely dark base to give the scheme the tension it calls for.

FIVE STEPS
TO TAKE THE CERULEAN SPLASH UP A LEVEL

The pretty, delicate and feminine scheme of Fiona Douglas's Glasgow living room has an extra Cerulean Splash twist that gives the room extra punch. An abundance of Fiona's floral printed fabrics are paired with bold artwork and all-over colour on the floors and walls to transform an everyday living space into a room that delivers a strong colour statement.

★ **COMMANDING ARTWORK** Either go for a collection of blue-hued pieces of art grouped together to create a gallery wall or opt for a single statement piece. For the former, be sure that the colours of each individual piece complement one another to create more impact when placed together. If choosing a lone piece then be sure to maximize on both size and intensity of colour for an instant wow factor.

★ **PAINT IT OUT** Taking a colour palette to the next level means utilizing as much of the surface area of the space as possible to add colour to the scheme. For large-scale impact paint the floor, walls and ceiling in tonal shades from the same colour family.

★ **MAXIMIZE ON TEXTILES** Cushions, throws and rugs are often used to reference more fundamental parts of a colour palette so naturally when you are looking to concentrate a palette it works well to double up on textiles. Here, an ombré rug and a sofa lavished with floral textiles invite colour to every element of the room.

★ **BOLD FURNITURE** Painting your furniture in corresponding shades of blue will pull each piece into the wider colour scheme; if left unpainted, they would act as cooling counterparts to the bold shades used elsewhere in the room.

★ **PATTERNED ACCESSORIES** Complete the scheme by layering in intricately patterned ceramics – Delft pottery is ideal for The Cerulean Splash – as this will introduce smaller details and points of interest to such a high-octane palette.

FRIENDLY FLORALS (opposite)
Designer Fiona Douglas embraces colour with aplomb in her Glasgow apartment: a tonal blue-green palette is used across the walls, art and painted furniture, with pink and yellow brights splashed across painterly floral cushions.

THE LAVENDER LICK

Wisteria *AND* RACING GREEN

SEEKING THE REALITY OF COLOUR

My only memory of a week spent on holiday in the South of France as a young child is the series of nerve-wracking hairpin bends on the mountain road that led to and from the apartment in which we were staying. So when I returned to the region for a long weekend in the summer of 2013, I was travelling with few expectations of what I might see. Sure, I'd seen the heavily Photoshopped images of lavender fields of Provence on Pinterest, but such obvious manipulation led me to wonder just how vibrant they would be in reality.

One evening I was driving to dinner in the next town when I passed the most amazing lavender field – I literally slammed on the brakes of the rental car, did a three-point (OK, maybe it was more like five-point) turn and drove down the dirt track that led to it. The moment you stepped out of the car the lavender's scent and colour washed over you; the scent was so intense it felt intoxicating and invigorating, and the colours were at once both rich and calming. Standing in the middle of the field all that could be heard was the gentle rustle of buds swaying in the early evening breeze and the gentle buzz of pollen-hunting bees. Drinking in the sea of purple all around me, I felt so inspired by the natural contrast of the lavender buds against their green surroundings. As the honey-like light danced its way across the gently swaying purple buds, I realized that it was one of the most soothing sights I'd seen in a long time. And this was a sight that needed no colour manipulation: The Lavender Lick was alive and bright all by itself.

PICTURE PERFECT PROVENCE
The sun-soaked lavender fields of Provence in the South of France were the inspiration behind the mauve and green hues of The Lavender Lick colour cocktail.

The golden hour light danced majestically across the mauve buds...

Purple is both regal and interesting, but it won't command the attention of a room. Play this to your advantage and layer other hues into a purple base for a knockout palette that oozes mysterious style. Try pairing it with racing green, saffron yellow or an intense red for best effect.

The Lavender LICK

MOODBOARD

This duo of colours is one of the strongest examples of how hues come alive in pairs. Whether you opt for gentle lavender or an intense plum shade, you'll see it soar when paired with deep shades of green.

Go bold! The racing green colour of this antique Chinese cabinet is a soothing accent to the dark purple walls behind. A flash of copper gives a sense of gentle opulence to the palette.

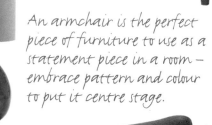

An armchair is the perfect piece of furniture to use as a statement piece in a room — embrace pattern and colour to put it centre stage.

A vibrantly striped bedspread is a quick and easy way to invite graphic colour into a bedroom.

SEVEN STEPS TO MAKE COLOURFUL DISPLAYS CENTRE STAGE

Displaying and arranging your wares is an enjoyable and personal way to bring colour to the fore in a room. Don't hide treasured mementos away in keepsake boxes or leave family heirlooms in the loft: instead, set them free, group them together and let your displays shout loud and proud about how much you love colour!

★ **MIX AND MATCH** A series of different textures and materials will give your display an organic and natural look. Embrace everything, from ceramics to wood and from glass to plastic, but be sure to use colour as red thread through each piece for a cohesive overall display.

★ **RIGHT HEIGHT** It's important to mix up the height and size of your chosen objects. By grouping pieces of different shapes together you will be visually varying the pace of the display, which in turn makes it more aesthetically pleasing to the eye.

★ **SHELF STAR** The windowsill, bookcase or shelves that will become the home of your treasured wares shouldn't be overlooked when it comes to adding colour. Make your shelves carry each piece with brilliant pride by lavishing them with your favourite hue. Or, paint each shelf a different shade for an eye-catching ombré effect to make them shine like the Hollywood A-lister in the room.

★ **GET PERSONAL** The best displays are those that evoke memories of loved ones, travels or special events. Work these personal curiosities into your vignettes to give added personality to your palette.

★ **BOLD BOMBSHELL** To really put a display in the spotlight you need to make it sing among the other elements of the space. A colour-block approach with a series of objects grouped by colour, from books to vases, will make your display a real head-turner.

★ **STORYTELLER** Each piece in your home has a story behind it, so embrace the role of narrator and use your displays to tell the tales of your colourful adventures. Maybe it was the animated bartering with a souk seller in Marrakech for a deal on that saffron yellow vase, or the amethyst ring box gifted to you on your 18th birthday? You'll be amazed at the stories your wares can tell when you put them centre stage.

★ **BE BRAVE** Displays are a small part of a room, so they are the perfect way to step outside your comfort zone and try something more daring than you're used to. A wisteria-coloured bookcase in the living room or a pair of plum and violet open kitchen shelves will ensure the spotlight is on colour.

As a sofa is often the most dominant piece of furniture in a living room it is well suited to bring vitality into a muted palette. Upholstered in a vibrant fabric, it will give the room a colourful focal point where the scheme is predominantly dark or light.

BOOKCASE BRIGHTS
Raina Kattleson painted the bookcase on her landing of her upstate New York home in a pretty shade of lilac, which smoothly offsets a collection of treasured ceramics made by her children.

GALLERY PARADE
(opposite) There's nothing criminal about the gallery wall that displays the spirited works of artist Mariska Meijers in her Amsterdam home. A rich plum wall and purple sofa provide a chic backdrop to the brighter shades that dominate her colourful art.

PATTERN PARTY (above)
The sofa in this Netherlands home becomes a vibrant colour statement thanks to a collection of boldly patterned cushions in a series of purple and yellow shades.

MIXING AN EXTRA KICK INTO THE LAVENDER LICK

Do you like your colour palettes as strong as your cocktails? If so, this intense mix of The Lavender Lick palette is about to become your new usual. The secret to creating this seductive and passionate take on the softer and more dulcet hues of the standard Lavender Lick colours is to choose a darker tone of each colour. The whole scheme needs to be more concentrated, so swap out a lavender sofa for an amethyst couch and paint thistle-coloured walls in a richer plum tone to give the palette an extra kick. The vivacious, saturated colours of Amsterdam-based artist Mariska Meijers's artworks called for a rich background colour to ground their array of brights. An intense aubergine colour for the walls lets the brighter and fresher green shades of her art sing, while a jewel-like sofa plays party to her floral printed cushions, which help bring balance by softening the dramatic palette.

THE MONOCHROME MAGIC

TO MARKET, TO MARKET

Taxis whizzed by in a blur of yellow and emergency vehicles screeched past in frequent flares of blue and red. All the while an eclectic mix of urbanites, office workers, tourists and seasoned locals navigated the rush and buzz of Manhattan's 9th Avenue. I was in the centre of a heightened sensory experience that was awash with colour, from cars to outfits, billboards to buildings and everything in between; this concrete jungle was anything but grey. Yet to my surprise it wasn't the red balustrade surrounding the street-side café, nor the bountiful pots overflowing with cheerful spring blooms on the central reservation, that sparked my palette-addict ways. Instead, it was the typographic signage painted onto the brick exterior of the Chelsea Market; its stylish monochromatic design cutting through the abundance of visual noise to stand out proudly from the street-corner location. I admired how the sign managed to command attention, almost as if the vibrant elements around the building were coloured accents to the imposing black and white background. As I was photographing the Chelsea Market building I noticed how the yellow traffic light paired effortlessly as a statement accent colour to the monochrome sign behind it; it was this unplanned dash of colourful wit that led me to create The Monochrome Magic.

When choosing the paint shades of a monochromatic scheme, be sure to paint each sample at least four feet apart so that your eyes don't blend the colours together. This will give you a more realistic impression of the differences between each of the possibilities, and, importantly, their likely effect on the rest of the scheme.

FABULOUS FAÇADE
The weathered black and white painted sign upon the brick façade of the Chelsea Market in Manhattan, New York City, inspired The Monochrome Magic colour cocktail.

BLACK EYE (top)
I love how the black and white filter on this picture I took of the London Eye emphasizes the shape and form of the wheel structure.

WILL'S COLOUR INSPIRATION
B B
CITY
CHIC

MAXIMUM MONOCHROME
A rich, matt shade of black has been used in this Norwegian home to emphasize the architectural detail of the building, while also zoning the open-plan space into a dining area. Cool white Eames dining chairs take their lead from the white floorboards to continue the monochromatic palette. Wallpapering the stairwell with a graphic pattern in a battleship grey creates visual depth in the space.

MOODBOARD

Nothing spells out timeless sophistication like a monochrome palette, but be sure to work plenty of pattern and texture into your scheme to keep it interesting. This palette makes for a great background to brights, so swap coloured accents in and out as your mood, or the season, takes you.

Typographic prints and graphic pattern bring visual interest to a monochromatic scheme – layering them throughout the scheme stops a monochrome palette feeling one-dimensional.

Introducing metallic details will bring an air of opulence to this colour palette.

THREE WAYS TO ACE ACCENT COLOUR

GRAPHIC BLACK Nina Holst adds interest to the monochromatic palette in the living room of her Norwegian home with a zigzag rug, striped cushion and cross throw. This mix of bold pattern gives the scheme enough interest to sustain its limited palette of black shades. A typographic print hung from the wall in an understated black frame continues the modern, graphic theme of the space.

★ **COLOUR BLOCK** To make a striking statement with an accent colour, introduce it in simple colour blocks, like a painted chair or tiled splashback. If you have a strong base hue, you'll need the accent shade to stand up against its colourful counterpart, so avoid introducing it alongside delicate or detailed patterns, because they will be lost in the scheme, reducing the overall impact.

★ **QUIRKY FOCUS** If you want the accent colour to serve as a focal point in the space make sure that it won't compete with any existing statement features in the room, such as typographic art or a graphic patterned rug. Start by considering the textures and materials of the space and then choose hues to complement their natural colourings. If there are no other interesting features, consider painting the skirting board and doorframe in a contrasting colour to the rest of the space for a quirky colour-led statement accent.

★ **MAGNIFICENTLY MINIMAL** Remember that less is more when basing a scheme around an accent colour. If you are using the right contrasting hue as an accent, you will find that a little goes a long way. Pick one part of the space to use the accent more liberally, like a statement armchair or through several smaller elements of the room, such as a vase, cushion or lampshade.

Accent colours are typically only 10% of a room, so when you are planning a colour palette try to remember the 60–30–10 rule: 60% base colour, 30% secondary colour and 10% accent colour.

MIX UP MONOCHROME The living room of this Norwegian home sees sunshine yellow accent accessories layered into a core monochrome palette of jet black and chic grey tones. Graphic patterns across the textiles add visual punch to the look.

MARRYING YELLOW WITH MONOCHROME

Monochromatic schemes are often visually striking thanks to the emphasis encouraged by their simple palette: patterns become more prominent, while the shape and form of furniture is more pronounced than it would be in a scheme with a more extensive colour range. Introducing a yellow accent to such a scheme will help to ease the tension created by the tight set of shades that form a monochrome palette. Nina Holst achieved this in her Norwegian living room by layering yellow colour accents through a series of finishing touches: striking triangle-print cushions and bold striped and colour-block vases ensure the accent pieces hold their own within the space, without overpowering the rest of the scheme. The key to success in using accent colour to soften a scheme is to match it in strength of shade and tone, and pattern and texture, to the rest of the palette – too strong and it will become the focal point; too soft and the accent pieces will appear to 'float' in the space as though lost.

PRIMARY BRIGHTS Bradford Shellhammer shows how a predominently black palette can be colourful in the games room of his weekend home in upstate New York. Bradford puts a playful spin on the dramatic black walls with a series of primary-coloured pieces. A yellow football table and red furniture set the lively tone of the space, while the bold type of the prints ensures the artworks hold their own against the imposing black wall.

make black playful!

THE CITRUS TWIST

A ZEST FOR COLOUR

Whenever I travel to a new country or city, I know that my impressions of the region's take on colour will take time to mature. Of course, there might be a sight that commands my attention from the outset, but an established perspective on the chroma of any given locale takes time to ripen in my mind. After all, a city, for example, can feel completely different by day to how it does after nightfall; the sunlight of the day can saturate colours beyond their natural pigments, while the dark shadows of night can make vibrant façades pop on sleepy streets. I like to walk around, often quickly at first, in a hurried rush for an instant colour hit; it doesn't take long with my magpie-like, colour-loving eye. With my palette cravings satisfied, I return to the areas, streets or buildings that pierced my memory most strongly, and I let the lens of my camera guide my natural desire for colour. I never fail to be amazed how the moment I look through the viewfinder I see a new layer to my subject. On first glance this building in Es Mercadal, Menorca looked like a simple Mediterranean building with a yellow painted façade. Then, as I studied the building for longer ,more complex layers of its colourful character started to materialize and I realized yellow wasn't the only colour story at play. I saw how the green painted window shutters were also central to the palette as they served to temper the brilliant yellow of the sun-soaked Spanish building. And so The Citrus Twist was created directly from the inspiration sparked by this building. Little did I know that the idea to create a colour palette by marrying citrus shades together, using one as the base and others layered in as zingy accents with a twist of black, would end up as the basis for my living room scheme back in London . . .

FEARLESS FAÇADES
The citrus-coloured façades of buildings across Europe, including France and Spain, were the catalyst for The Citrus Twist colour cocktail.

I first thought to combine citrus shades when I photographed this building in Spain.

GRAPHIC WHIMSY The living room of my London home sees a retro yellow sofa play host to an array of whimsically bright accent cushions, in colours inspired by a trio of screen prints; shots of graphic black pattern give a sophisticated edge.

The Citrus TWIST

MOODBOARD

With vibrant red, green and yellow at play in this palette, it's best to pick a hero hue and then layer in the other citrus shades as accent colours. A dash of whimsy also works well with these cheerful hues.

Vases filled with fresh blooms are the perfect opportunity to continue the colour theme of a scheme. In my living room I used cheerful yellow roses to reflect the vase and lime green chrysanthemums as a nod to the surrounding accessories; I softened the arrangement with delicate sprays of daisies.

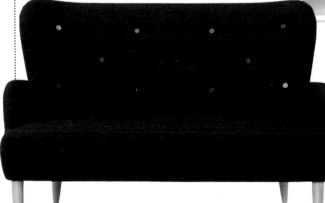

Black is an excellent backdrop for zesty brights, so consider using it across a few of the key elements of the scheme, like the sofa, rug or wallpaper.

SITTING PRETTY
Woodland-inspired animal cushions sit well with Scandi-inspired tree prints on the retro yellow sofa in my living room.

I love how the animal-motif cushions on my sofa bring a touch of whimsy to the living room.

5

FIVE STEPS TO ACE COLOURFUL ECLECTICISM

CLOCK IN The clock shelf in the living room of my London home works overtime putting in the hours to hold pretty for my colourful wares, from vases to ceramic cups and books. Yellow striped curtains and Scandinavian wallpaper give the room graphic edge.

Before you start to decorate a space, do you create a list with everything you'd like the room to express? I do, and I'm probably not alone in that list being lengthy at best. I was keen for my living room's scheme to express not only my unreserved addiction to colour, but also include my penchant for pattern, particularly stripes. Of course, I needed some playful, whimsical touches thrown into the mix, too. With so many colours, patterns and motifs at play, I had to strike a balance to ensure the colourful eclectic elements didn't feel juvenile, but rather sophisticated, with a quirky, spirited edge. Here are the five steps I took to perfect The Citrus Twist look:

★ **BLACK HAS YOUR BACK** Pull all your brights together by mixing some black into your palette. Much like white, black is great for offsetting colourful accents and has more punch to it than its lighter counterpart. Introduce black through one or two key elements in the scheme, like wallpaper or a rug, and it will anchor the array of hues layered across the space.

★ **FLIRTY FAVOURITISM** As a certified colour lover, I know how fun it is to flirt with various hues, patterns, textures and so on. However, it's important to pick a particular pattern to be your premier pick to reference throughout the scheme. I picked stripes and used them in the rug, sofa accessories, vases and ceramics to provide consistency. Break the scheme with one or two accent patterns, as this will loosen the look, but exercise restraint, otherwise the room could look jumbled.

★ **HERO HUE** Like every great band, every successful colour palette needs a lead colour to guide the rest of the pack. In true Simon Cowell style, I cast a lemon yellow for the lead in my living room's Citrus Twist line-up. I layered in zingy shades of green and red brights to support the hero hue for a chart-topping scheme.

★ **KEEP IT OFFBEAT** Even with an eclectic scheme you need to consider how you arrange all the elements of the room, especially when it comes to accessories. The key to a relaxed and easy-on-the-eye space is to either group accessories in threes, such as candlesticks, or layer in stand-alone statement pieces, like a vase. For the strongest look, steer clear of including anything in equal numbers.

★ **RED THREAD** The easiest way to make a colourfully eclectic room look stylish is to have elements that run through the whole scheme. This can be a colour, a texture or a pattern; I chose yellow and stripes as the two threads to make all the components of my living room scheme work together.

THE FLIRTY FIESTA

A Multi-Coloured MIX

FESTIVAL OF COLOUR

Having shared with you specific colour palettes inspired from my travel memories and photographs, I wanted to close out my line up of colour cocktail palettes with something that had a little bit of everything. After all, to me colour is about having fun and expressing your personality, and there's nothing more hedonistic than a multicoloured palette. But how did I find inspiration for The Flirty Fiesta?

The idea for the palette first came to me when I attended the festival of Sant Martí in Es Mercadal, a small town in the Balearic Island of Menorca in Spain. What was usually a quiet and sleepy Mediterranean town had come alive with a riot of music and colour to celebrate their patron saint. The celebrations saw fiesta horses doing the jaleo – literally translated, this means 'pandemonium' – where they were ridden through the cobbled streets adorned with brightly coloured ribbons and rosettes. Narrow alleyways and squares were festooned with multicoloured flags, bunting and string lights, and locals flung open the shutters and hung out of the windows of their painted yellow, pink, orange and green houses. Standing among the crowds, my senses quite literally drenched in a wealth of colour, I knew that I had to capture the hues of the moment. It wasn't until later that summer, as I was walking down the steep, winding path to the sea in Manarola on the Cinque Terre in Italy, that I decided to use them in my own apartment. As I reached the other side of the small cove, I turned and saw the tiny town hanging from the rocky cliff face for the first time. Each building flirted outrageously with hue, often right down to the washing that billowed in the breeze from the balconies – collectively they formed the perfect multicoloured painter's palette with their brilliantly bright façades. So go on, flirt with your favourite hues and mix up a party of Flirty Fiesta colours to create a multicoloured palette that is unique to you.

SUN-SOAKED SHADES
The vibrant festival of Sant Martí in Es Mercadal, Menorca and the colourful hillside town of Manarola on the Cinque Terre in Italy both inspired The Flirty Fiesta colour palette.

PERSONALIZE WITH PANACHE

To make a Flirty Fiesta colour palette work it's best to pick one or two core colours from one statement piece in multi brights. Too many multicoloured details will prevent the space from having a focus or visual emphasis. In my master bedroom I picked the yellow and blue hues from the headboard that I upholstered in a multicoloured striped fabric. Using these two colours across other key items in the space – the bedside tables took on the yellow, while the bedspread and curtains referenced the blues – ensured the headboard's multicoloured stripes stayed as the focal point. Finally, I chose to accent the scheme with hot pink via a framed print of a bougainvillea taken on one of my favourite holidays and a typographic throw cushion.

MOODBOARD

There's no palette more playful than one with multicoloured elements at the heart of it. The key to making this scheme work is to use one or two multicoloured pieces and then nod to the colours within them across other elements of the room.

I personalized my regular IKEA bedside lamps with a multicoloured bobble trim. It was a five-minute project but it took them from everyday to magical!

Multicolours work really well with stripes or patchwork, so look for interesting and quirky pieces to make the rainbow of colours really sing.

STRIPE DELIGHT (opposite) The striped headboard in the master bedroom of my London home became the reference point for both colour and pattern across the rest of the scheme.

In rooms with pitched ceilings it's best to paint the walls white to enlarge the space. Invite colour into the room incidentally through soft furnishings, lamps and furniture.

COLOURFULLY CALM
The serene white palette across the walls, floor and curtains of this Dutch bedroom is punctuated with delicate knitted soft furnishings and a statement headboard.

5

FIVE STEPS TO MAKE-YOU-SMILE STYLE

Your bedroom is a private place in which to relax, recharge and refresh after a busy day. This doesn't mean you should banish colour altogether in favour of an all-white space; rather, it's about getting the balance right and introducing the brighter hues in strategic places. With the right combination of soothing whites and energizing brights, you'll be sure to wake up with a smile.

DELICATELY DIPPED
The headboard in the master bedroom of this Netherlands home was made using recycled pallets painted white and then partly dipped in bright blue paint for a unique and stylish colour statement.

★ **CALM NOT CLINICAL** If you opt to make elements of the room you can't see from the bed the most colourful then you won't risk losing any tranquillity in the space. The headboard should be the most colourful statement, and then layer in colourful soft accessories like rugs and throws. Keeping most of the walls a soothing shade of paper white will make the space calm, not clinical.

★ **DIVINE DISPLAY** I'm all for proudly showing one's wares elsewhere in the home, but I think the restraint with display in the bedroom results in a more restorative space. A favourite dress hung from a pretty hanger, a few pieces of art propped against the wall are fine, but it's best to keep clutter out of sight.

★ **PERSONAL PASSION** Always include one or two personal mementos as part of your bedroom scheme. A pillow you bought from an exotic market or a map to remind you of your travels guarantee a smile no matter how early the alarm is set.

★ **MAKE IT EASY** Everything in the bedroom should be a breeze, so make sure there's a lamp within reach on each side of the bed with space to store your current read.

★ **TREMENDOUSLY TACTILE** Soften floorboards with delicately patterned rugs to make stepping out of bed feel luxurious not laborious. Lavish your bed with good-quality knitted throws and soft linens — we spend half our lives in bed, so it's worth investing in it.

go beyond beige

2. Graphic
accent cushions

1. Whimsical
lampshade

3. cheerful runner rug

in three quick steps!

BRINGING COLOUR HOME

ENTRANCES & HALLWAYS

WELCOME WITH A COLOUR HUG!

Across the world there are many customary ways for one to greet others – a handshake, a bow and so on – but I like to think that the best way to welcome a guest into your home is with a colourful hug. After all, in my mind nothing spells out welcoming, make-you-smile style like a bright yellow or blue front door that envelopes you in colour on your arrival. If you create a friendly atmosphere with colour through an initial space that represents you and your personality then not only will you feel at home each time you walk in the door, but so will those who know and love you. And if you're following the Bright.Bazaar style of decorating, your colourful welcome won't stop at the front door. Rather, you'll let that be a springboard for the palettes that wait in your entryway. Take the hallway of Raina Kattleson's upstate New York home as an example (opposite). Her azure blue front door is the lead for the entryway that lies behind it – the walls of which nod to the door with an all-over lighter shade of sky blue. This is the perfect entryway for her home because it instantly spells out Raina's no-fear approach when it comes to colour. Yet in spite of the generously painted walls the space is far from oppressive – it's fresh, welcoming and sets the tone for the homely vibe that flows throughout her family home.

ALL WAS CALM (above)
The hallway of this Norwegian home calls on shades of serene white for the ceiling and floor to utilize the natural light. A soft blue runner rug and wallpaper invite gentle colour into the space.

BLUE BEAUTY (right)
The entryway in this American home takes a colour lead from the azure blue front door with painted light sky blue walls. By painting the walls it zones the hallway within the open-plan space.

Using paint testers to create a geometric art wall results in a graphic colour statement.

TIP-TOP TRANSITIONALS

Entryways and hallways are often neglected parts of a home, as they are not considered worthy of investing in due to their transitional nature. However, I think that these spaces offer a great opportunity to step outside your decorating box and experiment with bolder colours, patterns and ideas than you would consider in your main rooms. As you don't have to eat, sleep, relax or work in these spaces, you don't have as many external factors to include in your decorating decisions. With that in mind here are three quick and affordable ideas to add some make-you-smile style to your entryway:

⭐ FANTASTIC PATTERNS

Use leftover paint or tester pots to create unique wall art, using masking tape to create geometric shapes.

⭐ PRACTICAL BLACKBOARD

A painted blackboard wall by the front door is not only strikingly stylish, but useful, too.

⭐ DUAL FUNCTIONALITY

Painted chairs give you somewhere to sit while putting on shoes and can also hold store coats and bags with shoes hidden underneath, helping to keep the space tidy.

CONCEALED ENTRANCE (left) Painted geometric shapes in shades of teal, mushroom and saffron create a striking feature wall that disguises a nondescript doorway on the landing of this Norwegian home.

SITTING SIMPLY (below, left) Layered red accents add colourful cheer to the cool white walls of this Stockholm apartment's entryway. A golden yellow fox sculpture is a nod to the walls of the outer building beyond.

BLACK BEAUTY (below, right) A hallway cupboard painted in blackboard paint not only creates a feature out of 'unusable' wall space, but is also practical for grocery shopping lists.

FLOWER BOMB (this page)
The pretty floral wallpaper in the boot room of this Swedish summerhouse is the reference point for the organic weathered textures in the space and the taxidermy upon the walls.

RURAL IDYLL (opposite)
Double wooden doors open into a glass and iron entryway-meets-tack room of this remote farmhouse in northern Spain. The space is big enough to let the outdoors in — literally, as the horses regularly peer in through the doors!

Inviting the outdoors in

When layering whites on whites – such as in the entryway to the right – you can use colour to add visual depth and interest. The Norwegian homeowner, Ingrid Aune Westrum, picked two complementary colours, grey and yellow, and introduced them across painted drawer fronts and mirror surrounds. By also working in some incidental colour accents, like artwork and accessories, Ingrid can swap out these elements easily when she feels like a change.

APPLE OF MY EYE

(this page) A smart palette of cadet grey and golden yellow injects playful life into the nook of this Norwegian entryway. A tall mirror helps reflect the natural light, while a console unit with painted drawers provides storage and a hit of colour.

NICELY NAUTICAL

(opposite) A series of ships depicted using string grace the wall of this Shelter Island home. The colours of string used for each piece are a nod to the brightly hued doors along the hallway.

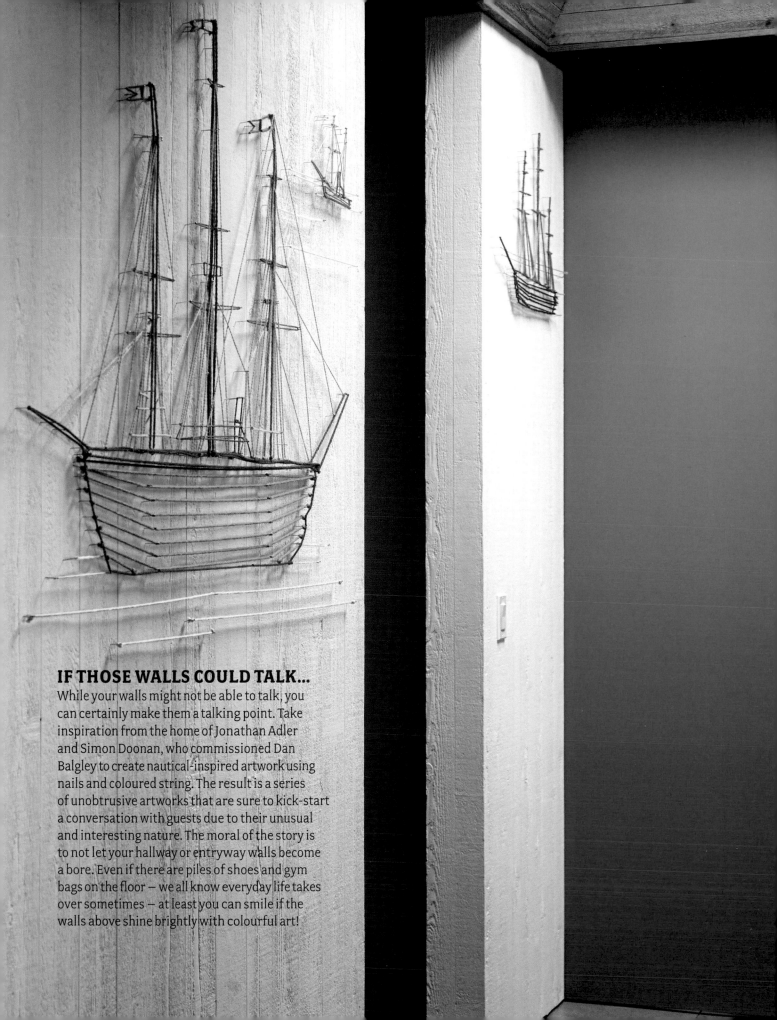

IF THOSE WALLS COULD TALK...

While your walls might not be able to talk, you can certainly make them a talking point. Take inspiration from the home of Jonathan Adler and Simon Doonan, who commissioned Dan Balgley to create nautical-inspired artwork using nails and coloured string. The result is a series of unobtrusive artworks that are sure to kick-start a conversation with guests due to their unusual and interesting nature. The moral of the story is to not let your hallway or entryway walls become a bore. Even if there are piles of shoes and gym bags on the floor — we all know everyday life takes over sometimes — at least you can smile if the walls above shine brightly with colourful art!

LIVING ROOMS

RELAXING WITH COLOUR

It can be hard to relax in today's media-saturated world, can't it? While we are lucky to have almost anything on demand there are times when a constant supply of emails, news and social-media updates can disrupt our opportunities to truly relax at home. Although I grew up with the Internet through my early teens, I still fondly remember the days before it became a central part of my life, and, frankly, the world. I would spend hours playing with a handmade wooden theatre that sat in the centre of the living room-cum-playroom of our family home. I spent much of my childhood dreaming of becoming a theatre set designer. When I returned from seeing a new production I would always try to recreate the set designs out of wood and fabric. Even then I felt inspired by colour and one of my strongest memories is of being enchanted by the exotic sets in a performance of *Arabian Nights* at our local theatre. My mum loves to tell the story of how I sat forwards, not moving a muscle with my eyes wide open in amazement for the whole two hours of the show. Perhaps it was that very show that was the catalyst for my lifelong love of hue? Despite channelling my creativity elsewhere when it transpired that my drawing skills left a little to be desired, I remember how relaxed I felt in our living room. Patio doors opening out onto the garden were framed either side by curtains with a pretty coral floral pattern that reflected the bright blooms in the flowerbeds outside. There were two pale mint sofas, an old wooden table with distressed, flaking white paint and a cosy wood burner that sat proudly in an exposed brick fireplace. It was gently colourful and instantly calming – the cosiest living room I knew. I use these memories as a guide for relaxing in my own living room as an adult – phones and laptops are swapped for a colourful sofa, piles of books and magazines, lashings of bright textiles and a scented candle burning. People say the bedroom should be the most relaxing space, but I also believe it's important to have one room in a house that encourages you to relax during your waking hours, too. In this chapter there is an array of styles and approaches to creating a relaxing living room but they all share a commonality – they achieve it with colour.

COLOUR CENTRE (above)
Painted wooden furniture in strong hues helps to draw the eye to the base of the room in this Spanish open-plan farmhouse living room. Placing the vibrant seating around the coffee table creates a point of focus and zones the area from the rest of the space.

COOL CONTRASTS (right)
The double-height living room juxtaposes brilliant brights across the sofa and armchairs against the rustic textures of the wooden beams and stone floors. Meanwhile a contemporary steel coffee table and bold striped artwork complement the weathered iron floor lamps.

TRIBAL TEXTURES The owners of this industrial warehouse in Copenhagen created a comfortable corner in their living room with mattresses covered in paisley blankets on top of old pallets. A generous collection of kilim cushions in rich red and orange shades ensures a restful spot to relax.

Add interest to white walls with a gallery wall of art that reflects the colours elsewhere in the space.

ECLECTIC COLOUR

The main reason I'm hooked on hue is because I believe it offers us all an opportunity to express our personalities at home through decorating. I love visiting friends and family at home and seeing how they've used the blank canvas of their own four walls to paint a picture of their lifestyle choices, inspirations and dreams using colour. The best part? Everyone's take on decorating with colour is different – sometimes it might be down to a tiny difference in shade or tone, and other times two homes can be polar opposites in terms of design. This, to me, is the beauty that lies at the heart of inviting colour into your home – it helps to make it unique. When I was studying at university I lived in a house of five and it was fascinating to see how we all approached bringing colour into our rooms. I created a nautical-inspired space by calling on rich indigo textiles and dressing the bed in exotic tie-dye patterns with a blue striped IKEA rug on the floor; a school friend and then housemate, Sophie, went for crisp whites and flashes of duck egg blue in her bedding and desk accessories, which was a nod to her sophisticated and traditional tastes; while another housemate, Jess, turned to her favourite hue, yellow, and painted the chimney breast in her room in the loudest, brightest shade she could find – a great reflection of her bubbly personality. So it ended up being a house of eclectic colour taste and it worked perfectly because the palette of each room spoke of our individual personalities. And the rooms on these pages do much the same: from the cool Scandi-inspired whites with layered brights of a Netherlands home to the rustic-meets-artistic quirkiness of an artist's farmhouse in Spain, each homeowner of the locations I visited to photograph for this book has embraced colour in their own distinctive way.

LIGHT AND BRIGHT (above) Anki Zilverblauw brings colour into her family home via a mix of pastel and neon home accessories and art prints. This gives her the flexibility to switch up her vignettes with different colours and seasonal pieces.

DESIGNER DIGS (overleaf) The upstate New York weekend home of co-founder and creative director of Fab.com, Bradford Shellhammer, and his partner is a lesson in how to marry black with brights. Primary colour is layered into a chic black base palette through designer furniture and quirky, tongue-in-cheek accessories.

ARTISTIC LICENCE (opposite top) Pâpier maché animal heads in a series of cool blues and framed upon a wall in the snug of this Spanish farmhouse tell a story of the creative spirit belonging to the homeowner's artist son, Javier.

PERFECTLY PAINTED (opposite, left) Amsterdam resident Mariska Meijers hangs one of her vividly painted works in a cosy corner, bringing visual bang to the empty nook in the process.

HANDMADE COOL (opposite, right) Designer Ingrid Jansen creates a cool and colourful vibe in her living room by combining one of her handmade reclaimed wooden side tables and knitted cushions with a vintage tan leather sofa and found home accessories.

WILL'S ROOM ANALYSIS
B×B
LIVING ROOMS

black is best
friends with brights

BRILLIANTLY BRIGHT BOOKCASES

I've always erred more on the side of being a maximalist over a minimalist; I find homes to be cosier and more welcoming when they contain pieces that tell the story of the people who live there. That's why I love bookcases – in a poetic way they provide an opportunity to curate short stories with one's colourful wares. I think of the bookcases in my home as miniature stages to create vignettes with the pieces that mean the most to me. I don't take my bookcases too seriously and tend to mix a variety of objects together – from the typewriter found at a flea market that nods to my love of writing to the ceramic owl cookie jar that denotes my fondness for both our feathered friends and sweet treats. This gives the collection an eclectic feel that brings character and charm into the room. If, however, you're keen to display lots of the same things, such as books, then you also have an opportunity to create colourful displays. If you order your books by colour, grouping volumes together in coordinating shades from the same colour family, then your bookcase will not only be practical, but a stylish colour feature in the room, too.

ECLECTIC MIX (above)
The industrial iron and acacia wood bookcase in my living room holds a variety of home accessories. From spare cushions to my favourite cookbooks and flea-market finds, the eclectic mix gives the piece plenty of visual interest.

COLOURFULLY COORDINATED (right)
In the living room of this Glaswegian apartment, a series of colour-coordinated shelves makes a bright feature out of a bookcase. Both books and home accessories such as vases are grouped in colour families to create a colour-block look.

ALL YOUR DUCKS IN LINE (opposite) The half-height bookcase in the colourful nook of this Norwegian home proves that organized shelves needn't look dull. A mix of magazines, box files and photo albums arranged by height and colour keeps everything within reach. A display of art, vases and objects on the top gives the piece a softer, lived-in feel.

Even with a
coordinating look you
need to consider your
colour palette: arrange
items of differing
shades from the same
hue, then accent them
with several items in
complementary or
contrasting colours.
Mixing in a few offbeat
pieces will loosen the
look and stop it looking
too staged.

COLOURFUL LIVING ACCESSORIES

Can't paint your walls? Not in the market for a brightly coloured sofa? Don't fear, as you can add colourful cheer quickly and easily using accessories as hotly hued colour accents. Why not pep up a neutral sofa with a generous line up of floral cushions in a series of watercolour shades? Or how about propping a favourite print against the wall next to a complementary vase? Either way, the best thing about inviting colour into a room through accessories is that you have the flexibility to switch up the look in a matter of minutes.

WILL'S ROOM ANALYSIS

B
B

FINISHING TOUCHES

CHEERFUL COLOUR
(above, left) I use this industrial sideboard in my living room to display a series of friendly accessories, from whimsical cushions and vases to bold artwork and typographic details.

PERFECTLY PLACED (left)
I propped this colourful print next to a blue vase to bring vibrancy to an empty corner in my bedroom – the colours work perfectly with the rug.

CRACKING CERAMICS
(above) A collection of blue and white Delft pottery upon a distressed teal sideboard brings both colour and pattern to this Glaswegian living room.

PAINTERLY PARADE
(opposite) Fiona Douglas layers the neutral sofa in the living room of her Glasgow home with a series of her own signature cushion designs for a soft yet bright colour touch.

THREE STEPS TO SOFTEN INDUSTRIAL STYLE

A rustic-industrial living room doesn't have to be hard and cold — with the right decorating steps it can be cool, stylish and comfortable.

★ **CURATED ART** Nothing gives a place personality quite like art — the personal nature of art choices instantly brings character to a space. Group art together to form a gallery wall that complements and tempers the harder materials of the space.

★ **LAYERED TEXTURE** Juxtapose exposed floorboards, pallet furniture and metal cabinets with a sofa adorned with welcoming textiles. Layer in soft, tactile cotton textures in throws alongside jute and grain-sack pillows to ensure the collection sits comfortably amongst its aged surroundings.

★ **RICH PALETTE** An industrial colour palette works best when it consists of intense concentrated shades with a dusty faded finish. Think rich ochre, racing green, saffron, rust and burnt orange and you'll be on the right track.

LOFT LIVING (right) A comfortable corner in this Copenhagen loft is created by lavishing a pallet sofa with soft throws and tactile jute cushions. A gallery wall reflects the textile colours to create a consistent colour scheme.

AGEING GRACEFULLY (opposite) A worn leather armchair is right at home in this old warehouse. Industrial lighting and intriguing artwork complete the look.

BALANCED BRIGHTS In the snug
of my London home I was keen to create
a colourful yet calm vibe. I balanced the
bold, graphic cushions and striped curtains
with soft, dusty pink walls. The gallery wall
continues the core pink and yellow colour
palette with a mix of my own prints and
those of admired photographers, and a
Jielde yellow floor lamp is the perfect
partner to the grey sofa.

COLOURFUL CUSHIONS

I have a confession to make – I'm addicted to cushions! Each time a new design catches my eye I can't help but bring it home to make it part of my colourful arrangement. This only adds to the handmade designs I sew together from my favourite fabrics. Because of this I don't just use cushions to line a sofa, I stack them in coordinated piles on bookcases and have them popping out of rattan baskets, too. An abundance of bright cushions in an array of graphic patterns, whimsical motifs and tactile textures means I can switch up the look and feel of a room as my mood or the weather changes.

CANDY SHOP (above)
The window seat in this Norwegian home has been lined with an array of pastel-coloured cushions; an occasional neon shade injects vibrancy into the palette.

MIX IT UP (below) A series of cushions from both my home and an upstate New York home shows how marrying cushions in a variety of styles, colours and patterns adds colourful charm to a space.

WILL'S ROOM ANALYSIS
B B
SITTING PRETTY

RELAXED STYLE Despite embracing a vibrant lime green wall colour in the living room of her upstate New York home, Raina Kattleson successfully creates a peaceful and calming vibe. Timeless monochrome prints and a country-style couch upholstered in paper white temper the bold wall colour, while a mid-century coffee table paired with distressed wood and metal side tables evoke a casual, thrown-together look.

OUTSIDE LIVING

THE BRIGHT OUTDOORS

Never mind the great outdoors, for me it's all about the bright outdoors – and the more colourful the better. I was fortunate enough as a young child to grow up in the heart of the English countryside. From the upstairs windows you could see rolling hills that went on as far as the eye could see. On the millennium eve my mum was working and my brother out celebrating so when the clock struck midnight my gran and I rushed to my bedroom window to watch the numerous firework displays in the surrounding villages and towns in the distance. The black of the night was alive with bright colour wherever you looked – it was a magical moment. The scene was colourful by day, too. A small orchard of apple, pear and plum trees offered beautiful blossoms in the spring, while country-style flowerbeds and a generous collection of potted plants on the patio offered colour in the summer.

I don't yet have a garden of my own, but I often dream about what it would be like when I do. There'll be different sections to enjoy, from a traditional cottage garden abundant with cheerful blooms to a more symmetrical Italian-style area, complete with a set of weathered iron table and chairs tucked away next to running water. For now, though, I'm happy to have an olive tree – affectionately named Enzo – that lives in a big Greek blue pot on my balcony; it transports me to warmer climes whenever the weather offers too many grey clouds. That's the great thing about outdoor space: no matter how big or small, it's the part of your home you turn to in order to switch off and escape the reality of everyday chores. Maybe you're the green-fingered type who loves to tend to your brightly coloured flowerbeds all afternoon? Or perhaps you're more in tune with throwing down a vibrant towel and soaking up some rays with a good book? Either way, Bright.Bazaar living is all about making the most of the bright outdoors.

LET'S HANG OUT (opposite)
The poolside area of Jonathan Adler and Simon Doonan's Shelter Island home encourages bathers to take a break and dry off in a hanging chair prettified with Jonathan's comfy textiles.

GET POTTING (right)
Short on time or space? Cheer up an empty corner of your garden or balcony in an instant with a brightly coloured pot full of succulents.

I love this approach to create an indoor feel outside...

Often the most dramatic spaces and palettes are created when there's an unexpected element thrown into the mix. One way to guarantee a colour statement is to play with contrasts. Try mixing preppy brights with a chic black base and you'll be left with a palette that commands attention.

CUSHION COMFORT (opposite) Create a comfortable place to sit and enjoy the outdoors with a seating area lavished with brightly coloured cushions – painting black panelling behind them will make the colours pop.

POOL PARTY (previous pages) The relaxing living room-style deck area beside the pool at Jonathan Adler and Simon Doonan's weekend home encourages lazy summer days socializing with friends thanks to inviting textiles and a statement hanging chair.

DRINK UP (above) Whether it's homemade or shop-bought, you can make a refreshing afternoon lemonade drink a mini event with playful melamine and nautical-inspired ceramics.

POT STARS (right) A trio of striped garden pots lend a graphic edge to the decking area.

KITCHENS & DINING

SPACES FULL OF HEART, HISTORY AND COLOUR

When I visit a house for the first time the lasting impression I usually take away is how the kitchen and dining areas feel. To me, these are the most important rooms in a home, because in many ways they provide an insight into the personality of the homeowner. These rooms are rich with history: think about all the important decisions made and conversations you've enjoyed within these two spaces. As a child you might have discussed subject or degree options with your parents while sat at the dining table; as an adult you may have broken the news of an engagement or pregnancy to family and friends while sharing a home cooked meal. There's something very special about gathering with friends, whether it be a large group or a more intimate dinner with close pals, and sharing food you've made together. I think this is why barbecues are so popular in the summer months, as they are group efforts – a few look after the meat, a couple set the table, others prepare salads and butter buns before all coming together to mingle over homemade food. My fiancé and I have always chosen apartments that offer open-plan kitchen and dining because we like to be able to chat with one another, or our guests, while we are cooking. Our work lives can mean that we are too busy to enjoy the process of cooking during the week, so we spend time together at weekends baking and trying new recipes – it's our therapeutic way to unwind. We make this method of relaxation part of our holidays, too. Instead of an all-inclusive hotel, we try to book an apartment, so that we can enjoy cooking at a leisurely pace without time constraints. I don't find cooking a chore; instead I think of it as a way to connect with the space in which I'm living or staying. And there's nothing more rewarding than cooking or eating in a space that's drenched in colour – just like the diverse and personality-packed cooking and eating spaces you are about to see across the next few pages.

WILL'S ROOM ANALYSIS
DRENCHED IN COLOUR

CASUAL DINING (above)
A reclaimed wooden table painted in a simple shade of white plays host to an eclectic selection of colourful mix-and-match crockery and cutlery in this Netherlands home.

NORDIC LIGHT (opposite)
Brilliant white floors and walls in this Norwegian home emphasize the natural light to provide a calm and cool base palette. This allows for layers of vibrant pastel and bright shades across the window-seat cushions, painted dining chairs and melamine serveware.

PERSONALITY CLASH
(overleaf) Bradford Shellhammer, co-founder and chief design officer of Fab.com, uses chalk on a blackboard wall to create a bold and playful statement in the upstate New York weekend home he shares with his partner. Exposed beams are used to hang pots and pans, while primary bright accessories temper the dark wood cabinetry.

The scandi approach
of combining cheerful
brights with cool whites
is my favourite look.

TOUCH OF GLASS
(this page) The glass panes in the hunter green cabinet in this Danish kitchen draw the eye to the red painted interior and mix of vintage tableware displayed inside.

INDUSTRIAL CHARM
(opposite) Worn wooden floorboards, racing green factory pendants and vintage wooden furniture create a rustic industrial vibe in this Copenhagen kitchen.

Painted blue cabinets soften this rustic industrial kitchen.

You can invite colour into a room without having to undertake any major decorating changes or projects. Simply pulling together a group of colourful dishes, mugs, tea towels and plates and displaying them on open shelves is enough to create a bright vibe. The key to making this approach work is to keep the rest of the space pared back and simple, so that the colourful display becomes the focal point of the room.

BRIGHT NOTE (opposite) Sleek, glossy black cabinets contrast with a distressed blue barn light pendant and a shelf full of cheerful pastel tableware to hit the right colour notes in this Norwegian kitchen.

EXPRESS YOUR SHELF (above) Open kitchen shelves offer you the chance to express your personality and show off all your pretty kitchenware. In this Scandi kitchen a series of pastel tableware comes together to create a bright and friendly display.

PERFECTING MULTI-COLOURED KITCHEN BRIGHTS

Don't shy away from brights in the kitchen — embracing colour in this creative space will allow you to reap the rewards with a cheerful and uplifting place to cook.

★ **SUITABLE SHADE** At first thought, multicoloured might make you think of garish rainbow brights, but a kitchen display that details a variety of colours needn't be loud or juvenile. The best approach is to stick to sophisticated and muted pastel shades, which may seem understated when used individually, but as a group they will shine bright.

★ **COLOURFULLY CONSISTENT** With a multicoloured display you are inviting variance into the look with different shades and tones. So to prevent the collection looking busy or visually crowded, it's best to keep the other elements, such as the texture and style of the designs, consistent.

★ **WHITE IS ALL RIGHT** The old saying 'opposites attract' couldn't be truer when it comes to white and brights. Pair these two opposites together and sit back and smile as you see how a white base makes your collection of multicoloured accessories sing.

COLOURFUL KITCHEN ACCESSORIES

Overhauling a kitchen is often an expensive task, and sometimes it's not practical to bring new furniture into the space to help create a new look. That's why accessories are your best friends when it comes to the challenge of creating a colourful new look in your kitchen. No matter how bland the cabinetry or dull the walls, with a series of vibrant kitchen accessories you'll be well on the way to a kitchen brimming with colourful cheer. If your cabinet doors aren't anything special, why not take them off to create open shelves? This way you can create a colourful display to be proud of, instead of hiding your best assets behind dull doors. Or why not turn your attention to the walls? I'm sure I'm not alone in having a few special plates that I rarely use for fear of breaking. Such treasures make for ideal plate walls — that way your crockery is not only safe and sound, but centre stage, too.

INSPIRED SURROUNDINGS (below)
New York-based architect and artist John-Paul Philippe created this mural around the cabinetry to reflect the views from the kitchen in this Shelter Island home.

PLATE UP (opposite)
Modern meets heritage on the walls of this upstate New York home, which, thanks to a quirky collection of plates and taxidermy, are brimming with personality.

WILL'S ROOM ANALYSIS
B B
DELIGHTFUL DINING

SIMPLY DOES IT The kitchen of this Spanish farmhouse lets its natural character set the scene — exposed beams and brick walls invite texture, while a pair of painted blue wooden doors and a red pendant gently lift the palette.

colourful and calm
farmhouse kitchen

HOME OFFICES

CREATIVITY IN THE FAMILIARITY

Working from home as a freelance interiors journalist and blogger means that my workspace is one of the key rooms in our apartment. Despite today's digital world, with smartphones and Wi-Fi that make it possible to work virtually anywhere, I feel drawn to the four walls of my office. I've never been good at working in cafés or libraries for any length of time – I always end up craving the familiarity of my workspace. I think this is because when I work surrounded by regular inspiration (things I have chosen to display and that feel familiar) and have practical tools near by, I'm not distracted by the sights and sounds of a new environment, which allows my creativity space to breathe. Of course, visiting a new place or taking a trip out of the office both help to fuel my creative spirit and spark ideas, but to actually be productive at ticking off my to-do list, I'm much better when sat at my own desk. Simple things make me work more effectively in my home office and they include: a scented candle to light on darker days or when I'm staring at my screen for a burst of inspiration; running my hands along the surface of my distressed wooden desk to appreciate the tactility of my surroundings; being able to look across to my bookcase full of colourful curiosities and inspiring titles I've garnered over the years; my Roberts radio quietly playing in the background to encourage occasional desk dancing and a series of my personal photographic prints hung on the walls to transport me back to times rich in new experiences and inspiration.

MINT-SPIRATION (above)
A mint typewriter brings a playful vibe to this desk space, while a single bloom and burning candle encourage a soothing atmosphere in which to work.

WORKSPACE NOOK (opposite)
The corner of this Norwegian living room is utilized to create a calming space to work. A blue factory chair is teamed with a yellow Anglepoise lamp for functionality and a string of fairy lights for fun. Wall-mounted shelves offer the chance to display pretty but practical stationery.

OFFICE DECOR AND STORAGE

In most of the places I've lived, the office has either been part of a multi-functional space, such as an open-plan living room, or it's been tucked away in a tiny room of its own. In this minimal space, there are pens, pencils, the latest magazines or journals for reference, creative supplies, books and personal mementos to find a home for. What is meant to be a practical space can quickly become a cluttered mess. I believe the key is to focus on creative storage solutions, making the most of every surface area– walls are ideal for hanging magazine holders or stationery shelves, for example. If you're worried about the room feeling crowded, opt for units with doors so you can hide your work away. Such solutions also give you the opportunity to paint the furniture to bring uplifting and energizing colour into the space.

HOOKED ON HUE
(opposite) I spend a lot of time writing about colour, so naturally my home office reflects my love of hue. I paired dusty pink walls with a refreshing mint painted desk and then added splashes of energizing yellow to give the soothing pastel palette a bright edge.

WOOD 'N' WOOL
(above, right) Ingrid Jansen contrasts rough with smooth by storing her extensive range of coloured wool in a distressed, rustic wooden cabinet that stands in her Netherlands home.

SHOW OFF (right)
A wall-mounted plate rack is reimagined as a stationery store in this Norwegian home office. Delicate patterns and pastel shades sit comfortably against the cool white wall.

PILE 'EM HIGH CLUB (left)
A floor-to-ceiling bookcase makes the most of the real estate space in this American home office and allows for plenty of storage space. Meanwhile, punchy red walls are accented with a graphic black and white rug.

SHELF STORY (below, left)
A narrow nook in this upstate New York home is utilized with a series of wall shelves for colour-coordinated book storage. An Eames rocker encourages impromptu reading sessions.

TWO TO TANGO (below)
A striking combination of dove grey and burnt orange result in a vibrant palette for the desk space in this Netherlands home. The colour match approach carries through from a painted metal chair to the desk lamp and even the stationery.

QUIRKY COLOUR (opposite)
The homeowner of this Spanish farmhouse layers colour into his office via painted furniture and accessories, including a turquoise crocodile head made by his son, artist Javier Requejo.

Turn to accent hues
when looking to invite
colour into an already
furnished home office.
By introducing colour
incidentally via painting
a mirror surround or
existing chair and laying
a vibrant rug upon the
floor, you will create
a bright and playful
vibe without investing
in new furniture.

WILL'S ROOM ANALYSIS

COLOURFULLY CALM

SLEEPING SPACES

BANISH DREARY DREAMS

When I'm talking with friends or clients about colourful decorating, the room that most frequently gets named as the space they are afraid to bring colour into is the bedroom. I can understand why: I've lost count of the articles that push the premise that a white space equals a soothing one – and it's true, often it does. Yet such schemes can also feel cold and clinical without the right textural elements incorporated. For me, I like to think that a colourful bedroom encourages us to escape to a place of joy and happiness – a respite from the everyday grind. After all, we spend so much of our lives dreaming that I can't imagine anyone wanting to have dull dreams. When you create a deeply personal bedroom colour scheme – a palette that reflects personal moments of calm and solace – then it can still be a relaxing environment if you stray beyond an all-white space. Plus, if the colour palette of the bedroom acts as a catalyst for bringing back happy memories then it will feel like a retreat at the end of a long, hard day.

In my bedroom I created a colourful scheme that calls on my love of being beside the sea. As I don't live near the coast, it's not possible to lie in bed with the window open and fall asleep listening to the sounds of the waves crashing against the shoreline. So I called on colour to help spark memories of these moments of pure relaxation and make my bedroom feel like a place of calm. From a multicoloured headboard (a nod to the candy stripe of sweet stalls that are so often dotted along beachfronts), I pulled out the yellow and blue shades as hero hues in the space. The balcony doors are framed by a lick of blue paint, and the bed is dressed with rich indigo and yellow textiles. Texture was important to the scheme, too. Multicoloured striped rugs underfoot and billowing, super soft linen curtains give a beach-house feel, while nautical-inspired linen cushions at the headboard lend a tactile touch to the scheme.

BEDROOM BRIGHTS
(opposite and below) I embraced my love of nautical colours to create a colourful coastal palette in the bedroom of my London home. A multicoloured headboard was the reference point for the blue, yellow and pink hues in the rest of the space. Linen curtains and cushions invite texture into the scheme, while framed prints and DIY lampshades personalize the space.

For a playful touch, update an everyday lamp using colourful pom-pom trim.

PEERING INTO THE PINK (opposite)
A duo of bright pink throw cushions are all that's needed to inject vibrancy into the bedroom of this Spanish farmhouse. A floral patterned headboard and delicate lace bedspread continue the feminine theme.

INDUSTRIALLY COLOURFUL (this page)
The intense shades of racing green and burnt orange in this Copenhagen bedroom prove that industrial spaces can be colourful. A brightly dressed bed is offset by a striking piece of art hung from painted white bricks and a lamp.

DRESSING YOUR BED IN COLOUR

The bed is almost always the largest piece of furniture in a bedroom and therefore it often becomes the focal point of the space by default. The key to making a stylish bedroom is to harness the bed's prominent status in the room and make it the focal point for the right reasons – reasons beyond its size alone. When it comes to introducing colour on the bed, there's no right or wrong – it's simply a matter of taste. If you're a cushion addict like me then you'll be forever changing the line-up of pillows that grace your headboard. If you are more of a throw-and-go kind of person then a patchwork bedspread or delicate cashmere throw to hand and ready to be draped over the bed each morning works equally well. If you wish to bring both colour and pattern into a scheme via the bed then it's best to keep the rest of the space pared back and simple. If you invest in good-quality, stylish textiles to dress the bed then a few simple accessories and a standalone artwork will be all you need to create a winning bedroom scheme.

When combining colour and
a frequently repeating pattern
across several fundamental
elements of a room, it's important
to keep the rest of the space
sparsely decorated. This will
ensure that the individual parts
of the scheme hang together
as one, rather than competing
with one another.

FLOWER POWER (this page) A
vintage floral wallpaper is the star of the
bedroom in this Swedish summerhouse.
A multicoloured knitted bedspread and
striped runner rug complete the palette,
allowing the rest of the space to remain
relatively pared back.

COLOURFUL CLOTHES (opposite)
Instead of hiding your prettiest clothes
away in the wardrobe, why not proudly
display them, like this Swedish
homeowner does?

One of the easiest ways to embrace colour in the bedroom and maintain a calming environment is to stick to soothing hues, such as soft shades of blue. Before you start to decorate, think about where you would like to introduce colour into the space. If you plan to paint the walls in a serene shade of sky blue then you'll be wise to dress the bed in pure white linens, with only a gentle splash of accent colour. However, if you keep the walls milky white then you have the freedom to introduce a variety of blues across the furniture, textiles and accessories. By ensuring that half of the fundamental elements of the space are left colour and pattern free, you will create a balanced, and therefore calming, bedroom scheme.

SLEEPING IN COLOUR
(opposite) Wood-panelled walls are painted in a soothing shade of blue to create an air of calm in this farmhouse bedroom in Spain. Delicate lace bedding is lifted via a hot pink knitted throw.

BOLD BLUES (above) The bedroom of this Shelter Island property creates a tonal scheme by using shades from within the same blue colour family. White painted walls balance the graphic patterns and bold hues, while a brass side table offers a touch of opulence.

SIT OR SLEEP (right) The purple armchair in this Spanish bedroom encourages the owner to make the most of his bedroom by providing a place to sit and read, as well as sleep.

BATHROOMS

SPLASHES OF COLOUR

Do you find that your bathroom is often overlooked when it comes to your priority list for decorating? Although this is a space that is used multiple times a day it often becomes a dumping ground for an army of creams, bottles and lotions, many of which are empty – I'm guilty as charged at times. Having everything crowded together ends up making the room resemble a looting zone rather than a Zen-like space. The key here is to create an area that's practical yet comfortable. Ensure you have baskets to store products and only keep out the frequently used pieces, so the surfaces have a lived-in but not cluttered feel. Having lived in lots of rented properties I have become well practised at injecting colour into the darkest and dullest of bathrooms. I like to use hues to prevent the space from feeling clinical. This doesn't have to mean all-over colour, but rather just a few brights splashed across the space through a vase, a basket or stack of towels. Small touches such as these are often enough to give the room a new lease of life.

LET THE SUN SHINE IN
(below) Balance dark walls by hanging mirrors to reflect the natural light. Jonathan Adler designed the tiles in the en-suite bathroom of his Shelter Island home, using their dark nature as a background to frame the intricate detail of his pottery collection in front.

WOULD YOU MURAL THAT
(opposite) Artist Dan Balgley created this striking typographical artwork on the wall. A roof light above the shower area allows natural light to flood into the space.

CHILDREN'S BEDROOMS

MAKING IT PERSONAL

In many ways a child's bedroom is one of the most important rooms in a home, because those four walls enclose the space where a youngster grows into the personality that will define them. Think about your own childhood bedroom: I'm sure you can remember plastering the walls with posters of your favourite pop stars or hanging medals and rosettes from sporting achievements. It's important to create a room that is flexible enough to evolve alongside your little one as they grow and their interests change. The room needs to have the adaptability to let them stamp their personality on the space. Start with the practicalities – kids love to have their friends over for sleepovers, so why not work two single beds into the room? If you're short on space, you could store a pop-up mattress under the main bed, but if the room allows a second single bed provides a place to sit and talk with children in their space. With sleeping arrangements checked off the list you can turn your attention to storage. While you might think you have a lot of things you can guarantee a little one will have even more stuff that needs a home. From toys and games to clothes and school books, children's rooms call for plenty of storage. An easy way to keep floor space uncluttered is to invest in a series of coloured baskets that fit under the bed. If you label the front of them it makes it easy for kids to tidy up and find things when they need them. Finally, try to zone the space according to their hobbies. Perhaps a crafting corner or a games zone with beanbags? Creating something that feels unique to them will make their room feel extra-special.

WILL'S ROOM ANALYSIS
B/B
UNIQUE SPACES

SLEEPING SYMMETRICALLY (opposite) The playful guest bedroom of Jonathan Adler and Simon Doonan's Shelter Island weekend home proves that a repetition of blues and graphic geometric patterns results in a stylish interior.

PLAYFUL PATTERN (right) Pattern takes centre stage in the children's bedroom of this Swedish summerhouse: wallpaper adorns all four walls; patchwork bedding hangs over the bed; a striped rug graces the floor and multicoloured weave baskets live under the bed for storage.

DOUBLE UP (overleaf) Not only does this Swedish bedroom double up on twin beds, it goes to town with pattern, too. It successfully combines a core blue and green colour palette for a room that feels lively and homely.

Children's bedrooms are great spaces in which to have fun with pattern combinations that reflect the little ones' personalities.

MAKING IT PLAYFUL

The best thing about teaming up with your children to decorate their bedroom is that you can embrace your inner kid. If you've always wanted to add a bit more whimsy to your home then a children's bedroom offers you the perfect opportunity. There are plenty of fun and joyful décor accents you can bring into a child's room without breaking the budget, too. Why not hang a cluster of different-coloured tissue paper pom-poms in one corner of the room? This will bring instant charm and bounce to the space. Or you could sew a series of throw cushions using scraps of leftover fabric to appliqué special words onto the front for a personal touch.

FINISHING TOUCHES
(opposite) Fiona Douglas added playful touches to the nursery in her Glasgow flat, with pom-pom trim on the curtains, metal toys and tissue paper pom-poms hung from the ceiling.

PLENTY OF PASTELS
(this page) A series of pastel-coloured elements, including wallpaper, lamps and textiles, creates a gently colourful scheme in this Norwegian guest bedroom.

When combining two strong colours in the same palette it's important to introduce some patterned elements to help temper the strength of the hues. A graphic striped rug laid on the floor or a bold floral pattern in the curtain fabric can work well.

HAPPY COLOUR The zingy combination of lime green walls and a Greek blue painted bed creates a palette that sings. Friendly floral curtains and a striped rug break the tension in the palette to create a room that instantly makes you smile.

RESOURCES

★ ONE-STOP COLOUR SHOPS

CB2 Hailed as affordable and modern design for loft, apartment and home, this brand offers colourful and clean-lined pieces for youthful spaces. | www.cb2.com

CRATE AND BARREL The grown-up sister brand of CB2, this store offers home furniture and all the accessories to match, too. | www.crateandbarrel.com

DEBENHAMS Look out for their designer collaborations for quirky design finds at high-street prices. | www.debenhams.com

IKEA Affordable and effortlessly stylish designs for every corner of the home. The pieces in their premium STOCKHOLM and PS collections are my personal favourites. | www.ikea.com

HABITAT Inspiring modern designs and quirky finishing touches for every room in the home – all at accessible price points. | www.habitat.co.uk

JOHN LEWIS Seasonal collections offer a mix of trend-led and adaptable designs that can slot into your existing schemes. A strong lighting range is available. | www.johnlewis.com

MARKS & SPENCER Great-value pieces across the board but their Conran interiors range is where the brand's offering soars. | www.marksandspencer.com

TARGET You will always find a core range of furniture and interior accessories and the occasional collaborations with high-end designers. | www.target.com

WEST ELM Furniture with clean and modern lines, an abundance of colourful ceramics, textiles and accessories and regular creative collaborations with independent designers. | www.westelm.com

★ FANTASTIC FURNITURE

BAILEYS HOME AND GARDEN An ever-evolving range of found furniture that will add a unique accent to a scheme. | www.baileyshome.com

BARKER AND STONEHOUSE An extensive furniture range that includes both classic and modern pieces. | www.barkerandstonehouse.co.uk

BODIE AND FOU Ideal for sourcing tactile wooden designs and furniture with a stylish loft warehouse feel. | www.bodieandfou.com

BUTLERS Best for rustic farmhouse furniture with a country vibe. | www.butlers-online.co.uk

THE CONRAN SHOP Expect to discover effortlessly functional and considered pieces, from iconic classics to inimitable exclusives and vintage style to contemporary designs. | www.conranshop.co.uk

CAR-MOEBEL Find wood, wicker and metal pieces often made by hand from natural materials. | www.car-moebel.de

FRENCH CONNECTION A must-see for stylish and affordable occasional furniture. | www.frenchconnection.com

FOLKLORE An expertly edited range of eco-friendly and sustainable designs. | www.shopfolklore.com

HAY Danish furniture that references the 1950s and 1960s with a contemporary edge. | www.hay.dk

HEALS The true home of modern and contemporary designer furniture with an impressive range of designs on offer. | www.heals.co.uk

HOME BARN A carefully curated mix of handmade and vintage tables, chairs and storage units. | www.homebarnshop.co.uk

HOUSE DOCTOR Every piece sold through this Danish brand strikes the right balance between form, function, style and comfort. | www.housedoctor.dk

JAYSON HOME Edgy but elegant and sophisticated not stuffy, Jayson Home scours the globe for a divine mix of modern and vintage furnishings. | www.jaysonhome.com

MADE.COM A great place to bookmark for affordable furniture that you can buy direct from designers. | www.made.com

MAISONS DU MONDE This vast website with an eclectic mix of styles is bound to have the perfect piece to match what you are looking for. | www.maisonsdumonde.com

OUT & OUT ORIGINAL Stylish furniture inspired by travels sourced from designers all over the world. | www.outandoutoriginal.com

POTTERY BARN Traditional American design with classic pieces ideal for country homes. | www.potterybarn.com

ROCKETT ST GEORGE A wide selection of rustic-industrial pieces and design classics. | www.rockettstgeorge.co.uk

ROOM AND BOARD Stunning designs made by dedicated craftspeople from across the United States. | www.roomandboard.com

ROSE AND GREY Find a contemporary mix of vintage-style furniture with excellent seating and storage options. | www.roseandgrey.co.uk

SQUINT Here you will find premium-quality bespoke and handcrafted furniture with an exuberant twist – ideal for statement pieces. | www.squintlimited.com

SOFA.COM A one-stop shop for every type of sofa you can think of. | www.sofa.com

★ PERFECT PAINT

ANNIE SLOAN The best chalk paint on the market – perfect for painting furniture or DIY projects. | www.anniesloan.com

BENJAMIN MOORE A vast range of more than 3,400 colours in gradually differing shades. | www.benjaminmoore.com

CROWN A more limited offering but offers excellent coverage. | www.crownpaint.co.uk

DULUX Well-priced paint colours to match every spectrum. | www.dulux.co.uk

FIRED EARTH Look out for their Mid-Century collection of colours in retro-inspired shades. | www.firedearth.com

FARROW & BALL Classic colours rooted in the company's English heritage. There's a wide range of neutrals and splashes of accent hues to marry them with. | www.farrow-ball.com

JOHN LEWIS OF HUNGERFORD Stylish shades from brights to neutrals that look good on both walls and furniture. | www.john-lewis.co.uk

LITTLE GREENE PAINT COMPANY A distinguished and high-end finish

from pastels to neutrals; great for heritage colours, too.
| www.littlegreene.com

MINI MODERNS Environmentally friendly paint that coordinates beautifully with the brand's home accessories and wallpaper designs.
| www.minimoderns.com

MUROBOND Look out for Mr Jason Grant's collaboration for a stylish, modern capsule collection of inspired hues.
| www.murobond.com.au

PANTONE Bring the brand's world-recognised hues onto your walls.
| www.pantone.co.uk

RALPH LAUREN Refined paints for classic spaces.
| www.ralphlaurenhome.com

SHERWIN WILLIAMS Choose from 1,500 colours, including those from a collaboration with US brand, Pottery Barn.| www.sherwin-williams.com

VALSPAR This brand offers an impressive colour-match service so you can find that perfect hue.
| www.valsparpaint.co.uk

★ ANIMATED ACCESSORIES AND LOVELY LIGHTING

ANTHROPOLOGIE You will find colourfully patterned and eclectic kitchen accessories and whimsical objects.
| www.anthropologie.com

ARIA Modern and colourful lighting with a solid range of design classics.
| www.ariashop.co.uk

B&Q For pendants to floor lights and everything in between.
| www.diy.com

BHS The Luminate collection offers stylish and affordable lighting solutions.
| www.bhs.co.uk

BROOK FARM GENERAL STORE A Brooklyn-based store stocking items modelled on traditional general stores but with a modern interpretation.
| www.brookfarmgeneralstore.com

CARAVAN Unique lighting options that will raise a smile.
| www.caravanstyle.com

COX AND COX Modern designs with a country flavour that work for both city and rural homes.
| www.coxandcox.co.uk

BARN LIGHT ELECTRIC Source factory pendants from here for industrial schemes.
| www.barnlightelectric.com

DEBORAH BOWNESS Idiosyncratic wallpapers that will always make a scheme soar.
| www.deborahbowness.com

DESIGN DARLING Preppy home décor and chic monogrammed pieces for stylishly minded, youthful spaces.
| www.designdarling.com

EVERYTHING BEGINS A wide selection of colourful finishing touches for the home.
| www.everythingbegins.com

ETSY Unique, handmade and vintage finds from independent sellers.
| www.etsy.com

FATHER RABBIT This New Zealand store stocks a solid range of kitchen accessories and storage.
| www.fatherrabbit.com

FERM LIVING Colourful Danish designs with an incredibly stylish children's range. Great for wallpaper.
| www.fermliving.com

FINE LITTLE DAY An inspiring mix of Swedish-inspired prints across artwork, throws, cushions and ceramics.
| www.shop.finelittleday.com

FINNISH DESIGN SHOP Extremely stylish and high-quality home accessories sourced from across Finland and the rest of Scandinavia.
| www.finnishdesignshop.com

FISHS EDDY Tableware and serveware of all shapes and sizes and with a quirky twist.
| www.fishseddy.com

FJELDBORG This Norway-based store is a great stop for colourful pastel pieces.
| www.fjeldborg.no

FUTURE & FOUND Graphic neutral pieces mixed with neon-bright finds and a twist of vintage.
| www.futureandfound.com

THE HAMBLEDON Like an interiors accessories department store but without all the unnecessary filler.
| www.thehambledon.com

HAYSOM INTERIORS An extensive range of lighting options, including both wall-mounted and standalone designs.
| www.haysominteriors.com

HEATH CERAMICS Beautifully handcrafted ceramics, from vases to tableware.
| www.heathceramics.com

HOUSE ENVY Rustic-industrial finds with a strong kitchen tabletop offering.
| www.house-envy.co.uk

HUNKYDORY HOME Quirky accessories and cushions with a modern homespun vibe.
| www.hunkydoryhome.co.uk

HUS & HEM A great assortment of Scandinavian interiors accessories for that Scandi touch.
| www.husandhem.co.uk

IDYLL HOME A beautiful assortment of rustic-industrial designs, with stunning lighting options.
| www.idyllhome.co.uk

JONATHAN ADLER Tongue-in-cheek ceramics, preppy accents and stylish metallic pieces from this admired American designer.
| www.jonathanadler.com

KHALER Graphic and colourful ceramics in varying shapes and sizes.
| www.kahlerdesign.com

LABOUR AND WAIT Classic general-store pieces ideal for a utilitarian scheme.
| www.labourandwait.co.uk

LAMPS PLUS The brand's Colour Plus collection offers more than 100 different lighting solutions that can be colour matched to Pantone and Sherwin Williams colours.
| www.lampsplus.com

LEE BROOM Eye-catching lighting from this inventive London-based designer. | www.leebroom.com

LEIF One of my favourite stores for colourful and unique ceramics.
| www.shopleif.com

LITTLE FASHION GALLERY Bookmark as a source for stylish pieces to go inside children's rooms.
| www.littlefashiongallery.com

LIVE LIKE THE BOY From playful to rustic, the boy, Ashley Sutcliffe, offers a curation of pieces from his favourite designers.
| www.liveliketheboy.co.uk

MARK AND GRAHAM A must-bookmark store for any monogram addict.
| www.markandgraham.com

MERCI The popular Paris-based concept store with an ever-evolving offering of stylish home accessories.
| www.merci-merci.com

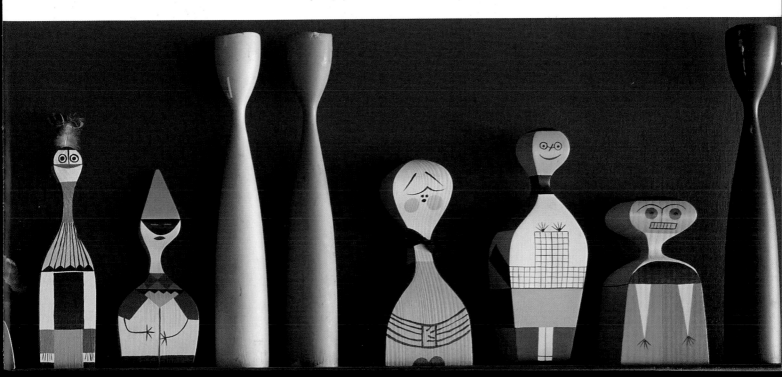

MIA BLANCHE CERAMICS Beautifully handmade Swedish ceramics in a range of soft ice-cream hues.
| www.miablanchekeramik.tictail.com
MOOOI Dutch lighting designs that create a statement.
| www.moooi.com
MUD AUSTRALIA Pretty porcelain designs with a smooth, tactile finish.
| www.mudaustralia.com
NOT ON THE HIGH STREET Curated by independent store owners and designers, offering a design for every taste.
| www.notonthehighstreet.com
PALE AND INTERESTING Delicate home accessories ideal for a soft finishing touch.
| www.paleandinteresting.com
RE Ideal for those conversation-starting pieces you struggle to find elsewhere.
| www.re-foundobjects.com
ROYAL DESIGN A one-stop shop for more than 50,000 home accessories.
| www.royaldesign.co.uk
SCHOOLHOUSE ELECTRIC An incredibly strong lighting offering, especially for industrial designs.
| www.schoolhouseelectric.com
SMUG Playful and quirky homewares, including a wide selection of prints.
| www.ifeelsmug.com
THE SOCIETY INC. An expertly edited collection of homewares from stylist Sibella Court.
| www.thesocietyinc.com.au
TERRAIN Organic and quietly stylish accessories for the home and garden.
| www.shopterrain.com
TOAST Timeless home accessories that are bound to become perennial favourites.
| www.toast.co.uk
TOM DIXON One of my favourite sources for lighting, especially the Beat range of pendants.
| www.tomdixon.net
ZIA PRIVEN High-end stylish lighting options for an investment piece.
| www.ziapriven.com

★ TERRIFIC TEXTILES AND FABULOUS FABRICS

ABC CARPET AND HOME A huge collection of rugs and soft furnishings across multiple styles.
| www.abchome.com
AURA One of my favourite sources for statement bedding, colourful cushions and eye-catching rugs.
| www.aurahome.com.au
BEMZ This inventive Swedish brand offers alternative coverings for IKEA furniture, as well as a curtain-making service.
| www.bemz.com

BOBO CHOSES Simply stylish cushions and rugs for children (and adults who are playful at heart!).
| www.bobochoses.com
BY NORD Stunning Danish textiles with striking cushions ideal for monochrome lovers.
| www.shop.bynord.com
CABBAGES AND ROSES Quintessentially English fabrics. Great for floral prints.
| www.cabbagesandroses.com
CATH KIDSTON Quaint and colourful fabrics with a homely country feel.
| www.cathkidston.com
COUNTRY ROAD Graphic and boldly coloured soft furnishings to make your schemes zing with hue.
| www.countryroad.com.au
DESIGNERS GUILD Look out for their stunning ombré rugs and fabrics.
| www.designersguild.com
DONNA WILSON Charming and whimsical animal-inspired cushions for style-loving children and adults alike.
| www.donnawilson.com
FABRICS AND PAPERS An online store with a vast range of fabric options for any scheme.
| www.fabricsandpapers.com
H&M HOME Find incredibly affordable and trend-led textiles for every room in home from this Swedish brand.
| www.hm.com
KAUNISTE Beautiful Scandinavian textiles that will charm you for years to come.
| www.kauniste.bigcartel.com
LUCKYBOYSUNDAY Find fanciful pillows for imaginative spirits and interiors.
| www.luckyboysunday.com
LAURA ASHLEY Fabric and soft furnishings for the traditional home.
| www.lauraashley.com
LIBERTY A one-stop shop for fabrics. Nothing beats the classic Liberty prints for timeless style.
| www.liberty.co.uk
MARIMEKKO This Finnish company is renowned for its original use of colour and pattern in fabric design.
| www.marimekko.com
MARISKA MEIJERS This Dutch artist offers an unrivalled mix of her vibrantly colourful and unique prints across various cushion sizes.
| www.mariskameijers.com
OSBORNE AND LITTLE A broad range of high-end fabric options in refined colours.
| www.osborneandlittle.com

PONYRIDER A great place to find cushions and throws with a unique look that you won't see elsewhere.
| www.ponyrider.com.au
TABLE TONIC A richly colourful assortment of soft furnishings, including an impressive range of Mexican Suzanis with hypnotic prints.
| www.tabletonic.com.au
THORNBACK & PEEL Unique fabric designs that play on artistic traditions inspired by a mixture of Victoriana and microscope imagery of the natural world.
| www.thornbackandpeel.co.uk
URBAN OUTFITTERS Youthful home accessories, including a range of bright and graphic rugs.
| www.urbanoutfitters.com
VANESSA ARBUTHNOTT Pretty and colourful fabrics ideal for country interiors.
| www.vanessaarbuthnott.co.uk
ZARA HOME Great for floral and feminine bedding, cushions and throws.
| www.zarahome.com
ZEENA Discover handmade textiles so charming they will warm your heart.
| www.heartzeena.bigcartel.com

★ ADMIRABLE ART

CASTLE Beautiful hand-printed screen prints, hand-stitched one-off embroideries and paintings.
| www.castleandthings.com.au
EASY ART A diverse offering of art options from canvases to framed photographic prints.
| www.easyart.com
FREE YOUR PHOTOS Turn your pictures into striking works of art with overlaid graphic and geometric prints.
| www.freeyourphotos.co.uk
JAYDE CARDINALLI Whimsical limited-edition screenprints from a San Francisco-based illustrator.
| www.etsy.com/shop/JaydeFish
MODO CREATIVE Order customised prints with your favourite saying or motto for a motivational piece of wall art. | www.modocreative.com

★ BRILLIANT BLOGS

My fellow bloggers will know there's a rich abundance of blogs available to read online, and will no doubt relate when I write that my personal list of top reads is far too long to be able to include everyone I would like into this small place. With that in mind the Mr. Bazaar Reads widget on my blog, www.brightbazaarblog.com, has an up-to-date list of my favourite reads. You will find inspirational blogs on

interiors, food, travel, photography and more, so please do take a look and hopefully you will discover a new favourite, too!

★ HAPPY HOMEOWNERS

Jonathan Adler | United States of America
www.jonathanadler.com
Lisa von Baumgarten | Sweden
www.baumgartendimarco.com |
www.lisavonbaumgarten.com
Fiona Douglas | United Kingdom
www.bluebellgray.com
Elisabeth Dunker | Sweden
www.shop.finelittleday.com |
www.finelittleday.com
Nina Holst | Norway
www.stylizimo.com |
www.stylizimoblog.com
Ingrid Jansen | The Netherlands
www.woodwoolstool.com |
www.woodwoolstool.blogspot.co.uk
Raina Kattleson | United States of America
www.rainakattelson.com |
www.astylistslife.com
Mariska Meijers | The Netherlands
www.mariskameijers.com | www.
iusedtobesnowwhitebutidrifted.
blogspot.nl
Javier Requejo | Spain
www.estudionap.com |
www.estudionap.blogspot.co.uk
Bradford Shellhammer | United States of America
www.fab.com
Will Taylor | United Kingdom
www.brightbazaarblog.com
Leif Thingtved | Denmark
www.centralhotelogcafe.dk
Ingrid Aune Westrum | Norway
www.fjeldborg.no |
www.blog.fjeldborg.no
Anki Zilverblauw | The Netherlands
www.zilverblauw.nl/shop |
www.zilverblauw.nl

The travel pictures I took for this book were taken on an Olympus PEN EP-L5.

All other photographs are by Andrew Boyd apart from the following:

All moodboard product shots

page 96, page 97 top left, page 98, page 99 Nina Holst

page 19 top : @ Dennis Frates / Alamy.

page 19 bottom: Camera Press / Bauer Media / Chris Warnes.

page 57: Mark Roskams Photography.

★4★

WILL'S FOUR BRILLIANTLY BRIGHT THANK YOUS

SANTORINI SUNSET
Here, I was reflecting on the adventures of creating the first Bright.Bazaar book while watching a golden sunset in Santorini, Greece.

After nurturing the words, devising layouts, poring over potential typefaces, sourcing and styling homes and perfecting pictures for a whole year, it's surreal to be sat here, in my cosy and colourfully serene home office, rounding out the final page of the book. I promised to 'work my yellow socks off to create the best book possible' and stayed true to my word — I managed to wear through two pairs of socks during a week of book shoots in Scandinavia! Of course, this book didn't materialize from my hands alone, so my heartfelt, warmest and brightest thanks go to:

★ **FABULOUS FRIENDS** Firstly to Tobes, my best friend and fiancé, for your unwavering support and for encouraging me to stop burning the midnight oil with our *Modern Family* marathons! Also to all of my family and friends, not only for sharing my excitement in this book, but for sharing a supportive smile when my confidence faltered, too.

★ **TERRIFIC TEAM** Thank you to Jo Copestick and Jacqui Small for giving me the freedom to create the book I had envisioned from the start, and for understanding Bright.Bazaar's ethos inside and out. Also thanks to Sian, Alex, Marta, Liz, Jessica, Sam and all the team at Jacqui Small for bringing your wisdom to the project. Hugs and high-fives also go to the US publishing team in New York City — BJ, Courtney, Nick, Anne Marie, Alice and more — I'll always remember my first meeting with you all on the 10th floor of the Flatiron Building on that beautiful March day. Thank you to my rock-star agent, Judy Linden, for championing my work from the get-go and for sharing your boundless guidance and knowledge — I always finish our phone calls with a smile! A big hug also goes to Paul Lowe for warmly introducing me to Judy. I'm grateful to Smith & Gilmour for understanding my art direction and patiently working on all of my late-night mocked-up layouts. Finally, a huge shout-out to my photographer, Andrew Boyd — I don't just have a new book, but a new friend, too. Working with you was always a breeze; from wild horses to burning buildings and more mad dashes from airport bars than I can count, there are so many wonderful memories to go with the beautiful photographs you took — thank you.

★ **HELPFUL HOMEOWNERS** Anki, Bradford, Elisabeth, Fiona, Ingrid A-W, Ingrid J, Javier, Jonathan, Lisa, Mariska, Nina and Raina — thank you for so generously opening up your homes and for sharing my love of colour.

★ **RADIANT READERS** Finally, a big, bright thank you to all the readers of both Bright.Bazaar and this book. It's always such a joy to hear of your own colourful adventures and inspirations, so thank you for following along with Mr. Bazaar. Here's to colour addicts the world round!